AUTHOR INC

THE ENTREPRENEUR'S SECRET PLAYBOOK TO
SKYROCKETING LEADS AND SALES BY SELF-
PUBLISHING A BOOK

RAY BREHM

JACK CANFIELD

DAUNTLESS

ISBN-13: 978-1-7327830-9-6 Digital
ISBN-13: 978-1-7327830-5-8 Paperback
ISBN-13: 978-0-692-81348-5 Hardcover

OUR EXCEPTIONAL CONTRIBUTORS

Foreword by Jack Canfield, Ray Brehm (Bookflix.tv), Steve Larsen (Offermind), Jeff Brewer (Launch Hackers Lab), Rob Kosberg (Bestseller Publishing), Emily Hirsh (Hirsh Marketing), Ricardo Texeira (Karate World Champion), Nathan "Rocky" Anderson (VP of Marketing Frank Kern Inc), Matt Stone (Buckbooks and 100Covers), Brian Berni (Bookads), Derek Doepker (Bestseller Journey Simplified), Adam Houge (The Fan Base Formula), Qat Wanders (Wandering Words Media), Sonya Wadhera and Priya Wadhera (Book To Boss), Albina Gabellini (Better Coaching), Eevi Jones (Influencer Outreach), Jeff Hilderman (All-Star Academy), Vera Mirna (Easy Button Healing), Elizabeth Hebert (Your Dream Esteem), Anita Plak Semprimožnik (Online Business Marketing), Laura van den Berg - Sekac (Bestselling Author: Get Unstuck Now), Lori Saitz (Building Business Relationships), James Archer (The Sharelingo Project), Ashley Emma (Fearless Publishing), Richard McCartney (Kindle Book Promotions), Agustin Rubini (Promote Your Book and FsPal), Jerónimo Cabrera Rocha (NLP Training - Conexo), Connor Boyack (Author: Tuttle Twins Series), Sean Sumner (Self-Publishing School), Scott Anthony (No Excuse Life),

Marc Reklau (30 Days - Change your habits, change your life), Alinka Rutkowska (CEO of Leaders Press), Kenny Yap (Life Academy), Paul Brodie (Get Published Podcast) and Eric Van Der Hope (Book Publishing and Launch Strategist).

It is not the critic who counts; not the man who points out how the strong man stumbles, or where the doer of deeds could have done them better. The credit belongs to the man who is actually in the arena, whose face is marred by dust and sweat and blood; who strives valiantly; who errs, who comes short again and again, because there is no effort without error and shortcoming; but who does actually strive to do the deeds; who knows great enthusiasms, the great devotions; who spends himself in a worthy cause; who at the best knows in the end the triumph of high achievement, and who at the worst, if he fails, at least fails while daring greatly, so that his place shall never be with those cold and timid souls who neither know victory nor defeat.

— THEODORE ROOSEVELT

FOREWORD BY JACK CANFIELD

Publishing a book is more than a way to share your message and wisdom with others. It's also a tremendous marketing tool. After all, no matter your industry or profession, everyone wants to do business with the person who "wrote the book." Becoming a published author positions you as an expert and instantly affords you the type of credibility that can skyrocket your career.

In 1975, I was going to school and working to support my wife and newborn baby. I was writing a book titled *100 Ways to Enhance Self-Concept in the Classroom,* and I only had 20 ways. I came up with a strategy—a blueprint, really—for creating the book. I wrote one strategy every three and a half days (or two per week). That equaled 100 by the end of the year.

The path that started then led to me co-authoring the *Chicken Soup for the Soul* series. The books have sold over 123 million copies in North America, with more than 500 million copies in print worldwide. But even that took a strategy for success.

Many, many people said that *Chicken Soup* would never work as a book. It was initially rejected by 144 publishers. When I finally did get a publisher, he said we'd be lucky to sell 20,000 books. The rest is history.

In 2015, Ray Brehm and I co-authored a book called *The Soul Of Success* where he detailed the four mental muscles of success and how you can learn them by doing stand-up comedy.

Since then, Ray has become a graduate of my "Train the Trainer" online training program, and is certified by the Canfield Training Group to teach The Success Principles.

Ray is incredibly passionate about helping entrepreneurs and authors achieve their dream careers. He encourages newly published authors to take the next step and create their dream business online. These ideals are encompassed in this book, *Author Inc.*

One of the biggest mistakes most new authors make is spending all their time and energy writing the book without sufficient thought as to how they'll market it. Ideally, you want to consider marketing issues even during the writing process itself.

This book provides the resources and tools necessary to create lasting, positive change, both personally and professionally. If you're interested in writing, launching, or marketing a book, or simply increasing credibility of you or your business, I highly recommend you continue reading what Ray and his fellow entrepreneurs are sharing.

Here's what I know: If you have a plan and the right teachers, you, too, can become a successful author. Best of Luck!

Jack Canfield

New York Times Best-Selling Author of *The Success Principles*™.

INTRODUCTION

Have you ever been ready for the next step and had no idea what to do? Have you taken all the courses necessary, but still feel like it's too complex?

If you have, then join nearly every other entrepreneur on the planet!

One of the universally fastest ways to get things done is to learn from someone who has already done it. Through another's experience, you can learn not only what *to* do, but what *not* to do.

What should you do right now if you want to start an online business, coaching business, or service business? What role should a book play?

That is what the experts in this book will tell us. You will find some amazing insights and detailed startup plans here.

Now, if you are like me, you are thinking that an anthology of interviews sounds kind of boring.

I hear you. I shy away from this type of book myself, but trust me: don't make that mistake here.

Whether you want to get your mindset on track, create a lead magnet, or create massive results in 30 days for a startup, you will learn how to do it in these pages.

If you are wondering how to go about reading a book with so much content from so many different authors, here is what I do: I look at the table of contents and read the most interesting chapter titles first, or those by the people I know.

But don't skip the rest! Every chapter has not-to-be-missed hidden gems. Find the ideas that suit you, and get started.

Or, better yet, reach out to the author of that chapter and find out how you can work together or get help from them.

The world is yours. Now get started.

1

AUTHORITY FIRST BY RAY BREHM

What is your business?

I help entrepreneurs publish books, become best-selling authors, and build authority.

What have been the key factors to your success and why?

Persistence and a sense of humor. Whatever can go wrong, will go wrong (and then some). But that is part of the plan. That is your test to see if you are worthy of the title of "entrepreneur." I try to push through whatever the obstacle is and laugh about it as I go. It is not always the easiest thing to do, but I know that is what separates the successful from the rest.

What is an unusual habit you have as an entrepreneur, and how does it help you persevere?

I am very visual. I need to *see* how things could end favorably before I start. That is why I like things like vision boards and sketching out funnels. Where I find the most bang for my buck in this area is book covers.

I almost always get the book cover created, as soon as I know the title, before I do anything else. I do this knowing that I will most likely change the subtitle later, so that requires a little Photoshop knowledge on my part (unless I want to send it back to the designer for an additional charge).

Having the cover complete allows me to visualize the book being done and motivates me to move forward. It also allows me to start marketing the book long before it is finished.

How have you used a book for your business?

In my case, my books *are* my business. I started out with a desire to learn how to write, publish, and launch, so I researched all I could. I helped a friend launch a business book, and that helped me implement what I had learned. Then I wrote a book about the process.

My books now are my primary marketing tools and lead magnets. They bring people's emails to my list, and more importantly, they pre-frame me to others before I get on the phone with them. It is amazing how people approach a phone call with you when they have seen or read one of your books. There is no need to convince them you are an expert; they've already made up their minds on that prior to speaking with you.

That is why everyone needs a book.

How do you make money from your books? How do you ensure this will continue to happen?

I make royalties, of course, but the majority of my income is derived from the authority those books create for me in the minds of others. When they have read one of my books and made a connection to some of the content, they instantly know whether what I am saying makes sense. That is a tremendous advantage for both of us, because it is a precursor to working together.

What bad advice do you often hear on the subject of authorship or writing a book for your business?

This may go contrary to what others are saying in this book, but the worst advice I hear is to get a publisher and to take two years to complete your book.

Quality is in the information you deliver, not how long you took to put it into book form. My most downloaded book—the one that brings me far more clients than any other—was completed in 26 days from conception to publication. That book was *The Author Startup*, and I simply decided to create a simple guide for people who wanted to get published. It was a hit, and readers can finish it in 45 minutes to an hour.

It is pretty simple to google the pros and cons of having a publisher, and I am not saying I will never use one, but here are the things that are important to me: speed, control, and marketing.

A publisher will make you wait 18 months to two years. They control everything right down to pricing to your book description. They will not market for you (in fact, they want to know how big your audience is before they will agree to a deal), and you can't market properly if you don't have control of the publishing account. I can't tell you how many people I have had to help launch who would have had a much easier path to best-seller if they simply had more control of their books.

Today, self-publishing is mainstream and such a better option for 90 percent of authors.

If you lost everything—your book, your list, your products, your platform, your fame—and nobody knew who you were, what would you do in the next 30 days to get back on track, and what role would a book or publication take in the process?

Well, first a disclaimer: This is what I would do now, but it is not what I did. It is so easy to see now, in hindsight, that I did not always focus on the right things.

If I had to start over, I would start with one theme in mind:

Authority First.

What I mean by that is this: everything revolves around your fastest path to building your own authority in your niche.

Mike Michalowicz wrote a book called *Profit First* for business owners. The main theme of the book is that you should always take your profit out of the business first, before paying bills or anything else.

I love the concept of doing what is most important to your longevity as an entrepreneur first. If you are a thought leader, entrepreneur, or business owner, the first part of everything you do should be to consider building authority in your niche.

The best ways to build authority quickly online are writing a book, appearing on podcasts, speaking at virtual or live summits, publishing content as much as possible, and building relationships with other thought leaders.

When I look back at that list, it is very intimidating. You may think so, too. In fact, in the back of your mind, you may be saying, *Yeah, I know I need to do all that stuff, but there is no way I can.*

I hear you, and I am about to make it sound worse. Along with all those things you should do, *you have no time to lose.* The only thing we cannot replenish as entrepreneurs is our time.

So here is what we need to do:

- write a book
- appear on podcasts
- speak at virtual or live summits
- publish as much content as possible
- build relationships with other thought leaders
- waste as little time doing it as possible

Here is the good news: all of this is much more doable than you think. However, we cannot single-thread these tasks. I am not talking about multitasking, which is doing everything at once. I am talking about multi-*using.*

In other words, we need to create a strategy to do all of these at once, just one time. That will be the most efficient way to get them all done.

When I first decided to take on the task of this book, I did it thinking about hitting the bigger best-seller lists, like *USA Today* and *The Wall Street Journal.* But slowly my idea about the benefits of an anthology book like this changed.

I tracked down Adam Houge to help guide me through the process. He told me from the start that the benefit of this book would be in the relationships, list-building, and sales. I did not fully grasp what he was saying until our first weekend of promoting the book, during the pre-order period.

We sold an incredibly large amount of copies, but the following week was unbelievable. My calendar was booked. I had people asking me how I knew all these authority figures, and my confidence changed for the better.

I had a book (albeit not my first). I was a guest on some podcasts, and I interviewed a bunch of people for my own. I was invited on multiple virtual summits. I was publishing more content than ever.

But most importantly, I was reaching out to my Dream 100.

If you don't know what a Dream 100 is, check out the book on it by Dana Derricks.

In a nutshell, think of the top 100 influential people you would like to have relationships with, and make a list. They might be Tony Robbins, Jack Canfield, Russell Brunson, or Brendon Burchard. Those are on my list.

Here are a couple others that are on my list: Rob Kosberg, Steve Larsen, Rocky Anderson, and Ricardo Teixeira.

Do they sound familiar? They are co-authors of this book!

One of the hardest things about connecting with your Dream 100 is feeling worthy, or that you have something to offer. But helping them build their lists or sell their products is something valuable to offer. Putting them in a book or a virtual summit is very valuable.

That is why I like the concept of a summit book: a book that brings in multi-author expertise and shares it. It is the ultimate example of a win-win-win. You win because it helps with all those things we need to do above. Your co-authors win because of the extra authority, list-building, and sales it helps them make. Your reader wins because they get an incredible amount of information from multiple experts.

If you position all of this as a summit and also a book, you may just get everyone you hope to join you onto the project.

So here is the 30-day plan I would use to get started. If you feel you need a book of your own, you can work that into this plan, too.

1. Create a summit.
2. The summit will also be a book (after the summit).
3. As you recruit and interview, document it all on your podcast.
4. Your outreach will be to ask people to be on your podcast, on your summit, and in your book.
5. You will also outreach to other podcasts as a guest.
6. Run your summit (and make money from it).
7. Publish your book.

This sounds ambitious, I know, but look at what you are doing. If you multi-use your content from the beginning, you are so much further ahead. When you get down to it, doing *all* of the above tasks is not that much more work than doing *one* of them.

Here are some details around those tasks. These are not individual days but the list of tasks I would get going on:

- Acknowledge I am in this for the long haul, and that I need to put Authority First.
- Define my niche and my ideal reader or customer.
- Write down my Dream 100 for that niche (prioritize those with the same avatar). In my case, those who serve

entrepreneurs (more specifically, digital entrepreneurs who need books, and are coaches, speakers, or course creators).

- Publish content every day (most likely with Facebook Lives, but I would reuse the content on my own podcast and blog).
- Create my concept for a book (including title, cover, and interview questions).
- Outreach to three Dream 100 candidates per day, and ask them to join me on my podcast, summit, or book (or all if you are comfortable asking). A pretty easy first ask is to invite them to be interviewed on your podcast. (You can start one easily on anchor.fm.)
- Document with video every day. Do it on Facebook Live, and later, you can sell the journey as a course (or a bonus for something else).
- Take all the interviews and build the summit.
- Take all the interviews and make them chapters in the anthology book.

In fact, this process is exactly what we workshop in my Authority Lab program. We create a customized, fast-track, authority-building plan, and then we start implementing.

So whatever you do to get started, just make sure to remember...

Authority First.

You can reach Ray at raybrehm.com or bookflix.tv.

2

LEARN AND IMPLEMENT BY ALINKA RUTKOWSKA

What is your business?

It's Leaders Press, where we turn entrepreneurs' book ideas into best-sellers from scratch. Of course, I didn't come out of the womb with this idea. There have been some milestones.

I started out in the corporate world, but I felt that there was maybe a deeper meaning to life than selling domestic appliances. So I wrote my first book, which was a self-discovery book in the self-help category.

That was in 2010. Since I had some background in marketing (it's what I studied), that book actually made me more in royalties than my corporate salary at the time. When that happened, I said, "I don't need you corporate guys anymore. I'm just going to travel around the world." I also negotiated a so-called golden parachute, even though I was really young. They gave me a year and a half of my salary, which enabled me to make that dream come true and travel around the world since I was free.

I didn't have to worry for at least a year. I could really discover what I love and do what I wanted to do without having to worry about finances. I started reading books. I discovered that I really enjoyed marketing these books, and I was good at it. I was sharing what I was doing online, and it turned out that I had a big audience. A lot of people were interested in how to market and sell books. It became a business of its own.

First, I started helping authors market their books, then, sort of organically, it grew to what is now Leaders Press. Here's how it happened:

At a certain point, I thought, You know what? There are so many authors coming to me with poorly written books, with books that are not positioned well and are in the wrong categories, and with books having wrong titles. These books are so difficult to market that I had to ask the authors to make a lot of changes before I was able to help them.

So I thought, What if I could take care of it all from the beginning? What if I brought in a team of ghostwriting experts to take those ideas out of their heads and put them on paper? Then I could come back and do what I do best—the marketing part—and that's how Leaders Press was born.

Then it was just a matter of identifying who our audience would be. We thought entrepreneurs would be the best audience for us, specifically entrepreneurs who are either looking for a lead-generation tool to funnel in more clients to their businesses or entrepreneurs who are looking toward retirement and want to leave a legacy.

That's how it grew, from the first book in 2010 to now. We help entrepreneurs do their books free from stress. We have had some pretty amazing clients. I sometimes look at the connections we've made in awe.

I wasn't born with all this knowledge. I learned this skill through a lot of attempts. I've also made a lot of mistakes and stupid decisions. I think you're either learning or earning. If you're not earning, then at least you're learning something that will help you earn later.

What is an unusual habit you have as an entrepreneur, and how does it help you persevere?

I don't know if it's an unusual habit. I have a pretty solid morning routine. I know a lot of entrepreneurs have morning routines, but for sure, it's still a small percentage. I do three things when I wake up in the morning.

The first thing is I drink a glass of water with lemon. You are dehydrated when you wake up, and lemon has some really good characteristics, like vitamin C. Some people claim it can cure a lot of problems. Basically, I like it. I like how it tastes, and it makes me feel good.

The second part of my routine was something I learned just a couple of months ago when I went to an entrepreneurs' event. A guy called Lee Holden was doing Qigong. It's not very well-known in Western cultures, but it's the number-one most practiced sport in the world.

It's the border of spiritual and physical. It's to awaken your Qi (or Chi), which is the energy in your body. I do seven minutes of Qigong every morning, and I feel really good after that. Since you have to move your body in such a slow way, it slows down your mind so you're not racing and thinking about a lot of things that you don't need to be thinking about in the morning. I find that extremely beneficial.

After that, I sit down for five minutes and meditate. I just breathe in and roll my head. I often list ten things for which I'm grateful. The whole routine takes fifteen minutes. All day I'm thinking about how lucky I am to have this awesome view of life—thanks to this routine.

I have to do this because I feel so much better, so much happier, and so much more effective.

How have you used a book for your business?

I've got three books on Amazon right now for authors. We have *Outsource Your Book*, which is the lead-generation tool for Leaders Press. It's where we explain exactly how we work with authors. This book actually brought us six figures of extra revenue in six months. It works.

It's also a lead-conversion tool, meaning when somebody comes to have a call with us after they read it, they're much more informed, and it's much easier to speak to them. They already know what we do.

It does a fantastic job for our business. My first book, *How I Sold 80,000 Books*, which I published in 2015, put me on the landscape of experts in the publishing space. This is also a lead-generation tool. If somebody likes it, they're invited to sign up for a free class.

Because you published the book, you become the expert. This is what this book did for me. You know, it put me out there.

Write and Grow Rich is the book that landed my co-authors and me on the USA Today Bestseller List. I've also got clients for Leaders Press who read this book and came via that book to us. I think a book is absolutely the best tool to generate leads and convert those leads into clients.

What bad advice do you often hear on the subject of authorship or writing a book for your business?

I don't necessarily agree when people say to write more books, because I think you should take the book that you've written and position it well before you even start writing it. Make that one book work for you. If you publish a book, you've attracted an audience, and you can create some offers that are valuable to your target audience that will allow you to make a little bit of a living.

I think it makes sense to learn from the books that you've published and marketed and *then* create other books. Now, if someone is just producing books one after the other, in reality, one is just writing the same books all the time because one hasn't learned anything from the previous book.

If you lost everything—your book, your list, your products, your platform, your fame—and nobody knew who you were, what would you do in the next 30 days to get back on track, and what role would a book or publication take in the process?

That's a fun question. I was just listening to a documentary, and the entrepreneurs were discussing what to invest in. One of the entrepreneurs was saying to invest in your education, because that's an asset nobody can ever take away. If you know something, build on that. There are so many books right now out there, and there's so much information online, that there's no excuse for not learning.

It's a matter of learning a skill and doing something for yourself first. When you succeed and profit, find somebody else to do it for. Once you have done that, you have your first testimonial. Take that to market. We will put together the funnel. If I started from scratch, I would ask myself the questions, *What do I want to do that will make me happy? What am I passionate about?* If it's book marketing, I'm learning more and more about that to do my own book launch.

When I see that that's working, I do it for somebody else. Then I'd start attracting people into my business to do books and book launchings. I think that's the simple answer.

I think it's really important to read and apply—read and apply. Rather than read twenty books and do nothing, read twenty pages and *do something*. There is so much knowledge in books, and I know I'm biased because we do books for entrepreneurs, but I learned how to evaluate and hire people thanks to books.

One of my team members sent me a book on hiring. What I learned from this book was worth thousands of dollars to me in my business. More importantly, what I learned from this book could be packaged and sold as a system—for thousands of dollars.

I can teach others how to hire people and create a workshop. I read a nine-dollar book, and now I have a system. It's just amazing what you can learn through books, and it's never been easier. You see a book on Amazon, and you get it immediately on your Kindle.

It's no longer an issue of *how* to access knowledge.

It's a matter of *implementing*.

Read a little bit, implement a little bit, and you're going to learn. You're going to hone your own skills, create your own system, then be able to add a lot of value to other people's lives just like we do at Leaders Press.

You can reach Alinka at leaderspress.com.

3

GET MORE VISIBILITY BY ADAM HOUGE

What is your business?

I help entrepreneurs grow their audiences and profitability.

Ultimately, a big part of that group ends up becoming authors. That's where I got my start selling books. Authors have a deep need to get more visibility, more eyes on their books, to sell more copies. That's what led me into this realm of helping and teaching others, not only how to sell more, but to hit major best-seller lists.

What have been the key factors to your success and why?

Go get more knowledge. I've always had a constant drive to pursue passionately how to get things to work, and in this case, what I was pursuing when I first started out was how to get more visibility for the books I had written. At first, I started looking at Google—how can I use their search engine? You want to have the warmest traffic possible, and warm traffic needs to also be interested traffic. Warm traffic consists of people who would like to buy now and people who are interested in what you're selling. Everything kept coming back to Amazon and their recommendation engines, because they have so much traffic. The reason they're doing a search on Amazon is to find a book exactly like yours.

When I came to that realization, I started trying to find more accurately how their algorithm actually worked. As I began to discover the process of how to connect with my potential fans and readers through Amazon, it helped me to understand what they were looking for in promotional patterns. That ultimately comes to what launches need to look like. I began studying more about book launches, and they helped me to connect to the algorithm. Ironically, the way a really good, solid *New York Times* best-selling book launch would look is how a six-figure course or high-ticket product would launch. Long story short, that is what led me to what I now know and what I now do.

What is an unusual habit you have as an entrepreneur, and how does it help you persevere?

I like raising animals, but that has nothing to do with entrepreneurship. I've got some ducks right now. I took in some kittens.

What has helped me are more of the mental habits. That's what I want to steer people toward. The way you think can help you with decisions. Everything that you are in your life is a combination of all the decisions you've already made. If you are able to make all the accurate decisions, you could not only have a more successful life but a happier life.

Learn more, know yourself, know your limitations, understand, have humility. Some of the most successful people I've ever encountered have incredible humility. It really comes down to that mentality of looking toward people who are successful and asking yourself what they have done to get there. When you understand that process, break it down into the simplest steps. What do you need to do today?

I have a habit of trying to look for the opportunity and the positivity in circumstances. When something goes wrong, I say, this is a learning lesson. There is something that works because Joe or Sandy over here are able to get it to work. What have they done differently? How can I humble myself in this situation? There's something that needs to work. Pinpoint it, figure it out, and fix it.

How have you used a book your business?

I used to depend solely on book income. We're talking like $15 in my first month, but before long, I'd grown to generating six figures. I began to realize there's more of a process here for growth—you're going to hit certain ceilings when the only thing you're doing is sitting on an algorithm. They can only get you to a certain height in your business. I wanted to grow beyond these borders that I created for myself. Granted, they were six-figure borders, which most people would be happy and content with. It wasn't really about money for me; it was about reaching more people. Ultimately, that's what my main passion has always been.

How can I touch more lives? How can I change people? What can I do to bring out their best? It's always come full circle to a concept that ultimately causes more sales. I was looking for ways to get in front of more eyes, so, over time, what I ended up doing was creating online courses, high-ticket programs, etc. An important part in that is they are fantastic audience builders. Depending on what your audience is looking for, some of those might bring in more people per dollar spent than on an ad.

The difference is evangelism. When somebody reads your book, you, in essence, are evangelizing them to a concept you personally are teaching. When they have been brought through this onboarding process, it's not just seeing your knowledge but falling in love with the concept of what you're teaching. You're able to show them better opportunities—also known as online courses and high-ticket programs—in order to work with you. I have found that through books—due to this process of onboarding, evangelism, etc.—it has allowed me to have higher sales per subscriber than most other people.

How do you make money from your books? How do you ensure this will continue to happen?

Continue to put out more free content. Not everybody can afford to pay you today, but when they can, they will. They want to invest in themselves. You should not look at people like a dollar sign. Now, obviously there is an element of business, but you must remember your subscribers are human beings. If you're trying to transform their lives, you need to be willing to become an asset to their lives.

When I do a webinar, I don't ever set one up that's salesy and sleazy. I don't believe in that. I want them to be able to walk away with an actionable step-by-step formula that they can get some serious results with, because the more results people get, the more they're going to realize you're the real deal. It's going to build trust and favor. These are the kinds of things you need to do in order to entertain, build a fan base, and then entertain that fan base.

I have given very much away for free—but I have made so much money off it. I help so many different people, and I love it. I absolutely love it. I find it to be the best model out there.

What bad advice do you often hear on the subject of authorship or writing a book for your business?

I hear some people saying to sell your book at $2.99 or $4.99 during your launch. That's pretty high. You want to have launches that are cheaper because Amazon does not give you traction based on cost. They give you traction based on quantity of sales.

Once you are higher on the algorithm, you can raise your price. During the launch, I usually recommend pricing at $0.99, then, once the launch is over, raise it to full price—whatever it might be. That's going to help you sit higher for longer on their algorithms—so long as your categories and keywords are correct there. I've also seen people say to do long-tail keywords. The traffic is so small on Amazon for long-tail keywords, it's ridiculous. You want to do things that are focused and ask yourself, what are people looking for right now? Right here?

They don't give enough attention to audience growth. They don't give enough attention to giving away free material to their audience to really build them. It's such an interesting world, the internet, because people act more personable. We have social media and so many different ways of connecting—Facebook, Twitter, Youtube. People expect you to just be you. I recommend having a professional image, but it should be the best version of you. And care about people.

Another big part of bad advice I see is people just telling you to chase after dollar signs. The more you do that, the less people will trust you. If you can have a student who has experienced real transformation, they immediately become a testimonial. The more testimonials you have, the more people will see you do care about them. People want someone to take them by the hand and care about them as an individual to help them meet their goals. That's what they're looking to pay for. Be that person, but not for the reason of profit. Be genuine.

If you lost everything—your book, your list, your products, your platform, your fame—and nobody knew who you were, what would you do in the next 30 days to get back on track, and what role would a book or publication take in the process?

I would write a very short book in a couple of days and send that over to an editor—get it done, get a good cover made, make it beautiful. I would not sell it in stores. I would start shaking hands, trying to meet partners, and I would try to put together a high-ticket program and a training (the course I'd use as a freebie to get people in the door). I would train them with a free program—a recording, a webinar—and then I would use that to send them to a high ticket.

Then I would leverage other people's audiences. I wouldn't worry about whether I have an audience or not. You'd be surprised how many people would work with you if you schedule something as a launch. Get three to five people willing to promote you. Now you've given yourself a way to grow your audience enough to cross-promote them, and you could get a couple thousand from that. Well, you might have to send out more emails than they sent because your audience is currently smaller, but it gives you a way to grow quickly.

That's what I will do. That's just starting out over time. If I lost everything I have now, I would take the knowledge I know in launching, and, over time, I would build that. My one-year plan would be putting together a USA Today launch. Prestige is a powerful thing, and people are drawn to it from a business perspective. Even if you don't hit the lists, people are promoting themselves in your book while promoting you, and they're more likely to work with you in the future. Then you can leverage their audiences and expand through partnerships with them and their friends, their partners. There is a huge network to always be able to get involved in.

You can reach Adam at thefanbaseformula.com.

4

ONE GOOD CLIENT IS ALL IT TAKES BY ROB KOSBERG

What is your business?

Bestseller Publishing Business. We help entrepreneurs, experts, coaches, consultants, and brick-and-mortar business owners to ghost-write and publish a book through the Big Marketing Push Book Launch Forum. We have PR and media teams. We work with them on TV, radio, all that—even help them write the book if they need it. We focus in the nonfiction space for the expert industry.

What have been the key factors to your success and why?

My company, Book Funnel, is now crushing it. It has probably generated $3 million in revenue already this year. Sales and revenue. It's just doing fantastic. When I got started, I backed into it by writing a book for my financial services company, going back 11 years ago now. Little by little, I ended up selling that company and transitioning. It's all revolving around a book.

What is an unusual habit you have as an entrepreneur, and how does it help you persevere?

My morning routine, which is set in stone and rock solid. I wasn't always a particularly disciplined person growing up, but I understood the importance of it and really wanted to develop discipline in my life, even as a younger man. And now, in my 50s, I'm in a rock-solid morning routine. I got a dog that wakes me up. He's got to go for a walk before six, so we're up at five. Usually, I make my bulletproof coffee, and we're walking by 5:30, then I have my time of meditation and reading. All that stuff just sets my mind. I work out not quite every day, but about five days a week in the morning. Morning routine makes all the difference for me.

I like routine—some people don't, but I do. I like having things to look forward to every day in my schedule. I know the calls I have. I live on my calendar. I like that; that, to me, feels right. I know some people hate that. A good friend of mine, Dean Jackson, just doesn't want to live that way at all and has built his life around not doing it. I guess it's just different strokes, right?

I like my calendar. I like when it's wide open—"wide open" for me means I blocked the whole thing out with something. "Wide open" for me means it's filled with, like, my Thursday golf or whatever.

How have you used a book for your business?

Let's go back 11 years. I didn't know what I was doing then. I know what I'm doing now, but 11 years ago, when I wrote that financial services book, I knew I needed to get the book in front of people. If you go back 11 years, you know that's 2008, which was a horrible time. It was the height of the recession, and the stock market had dumped 50 percent. Real estate had dumped 50 to 60 percent in certain areas.

I used my book and got on the radio. I used radio in conjunction with offering my book for free to get people to call or to go on my website and fill out a kind of archaic form from 11 years ago. And so, in some ways, it's no different. I mean, that was, I guess, the makings of a funnel—kind of the makings of a free-plus-shipping, although shipping was free, too. I didn't know to actually charge for shipping in those days. No one told me. So we would actually ship the book for free. But you know, it's book-plus-audience-equals-results, and an obviously ideal audience equals results.

I had the very first book funnel—a radio book funnel. I kind of put two and two together. What could be better than somebody wanting my book when it's clearly for people that I can help? I mean, it just seemed like an obvious thing.

How do you make money from your books? How do you ensure this will continue to happen?

I actually just talked about that today on my BSB coaching call. How do I make money? I make money because I have a high-ticket offer. Our focus is nonfiction expert space. If I'm doing a book for somebody writing on a cryptocurrency, he might be able to sell a lot of books, but his money is going to be made elsewhere. It's going to be made in selling higher ticket programs, products, courses, and even coaching, maybe getting them into a monthly community where he shows them how he does his trading and all of that stuff.

And the same is true for us. We have a high-ticket service. I can get a lot of these books into people's hands because of the level of service on the back end. If you don't have that, you are massively handicapped. That's what I tell people. We lose a lot of potentially good clients by just being brutally honest. If they don't have a back-end offer, they're probably not going to make a lot of money. That's just the truth. You got to have the back-end offer. If you have that, then there's a lot of money and opportunity to use a book to drive people to it.

How would I ensure that that keeps happening? By repurposing content. This is nothing more than my repurposing the content from this book into the form of questions and forms for people to fill out. That's all. There's nothing new written. So, if you're not willing to write new content, then find a way to repurpose your older content and keep things fresh.

What bad advice do you often hear on the subject of authorship or writing a book for your business?

There's a lot of bad advice. Many times, experts say, you just need to start writing, or you need to write every single day. That's a little like saying, to build a skyscraper, you just need to start throwing bricks in a pile, and it's going to pop up. I mean, eventually it'll be a monument to the heavens—the Tower of Babel. You wouldn't do anything worthwhile so haphazardly, so you can't just write through the thinking stage. You have to think it through and build out the foundation first.

The other thing I hear a good deal, which is terrifying, is that people can write books to become experts. You can write a book and become an authority or a thought leader. You're an authority or thought leader because of the attention the book gets you. But some people come to us and want to write a book but don't have any knowledge of the subject. They ask us, will you do research on it? No, you're supposed to be the expert. We're writing about your expertise, not creating something out of thin air. I have seen many people talk about starting a business from scratch. I mean, there are a whole lot of book businesses built around people that have very little in the way of expertise or real working knowledge of their subject. They're writing books on it, and all of a sudden, they're "experts."

No, you're really not.

There are courses and programs that actually will help you to do that. I just think it's a disservice to everybody. It's a disservice to the individual. It's a disservice to the people that individual may convince to get to work with them. Anybody who teaches that would say, well, that's not what we teach. We want people that have a real working knowledge. I'm not here to speak badly about what anybody else is doing, but I have heard that advice, and I have seen programs built around that. All I would say is, look, learn your craft, learn your expertise first, and, from there, use a book to blow it up.

If you lost everything—your book, your list, your products, your platform, your fame—and nobody knew who you were, what would you do in the next 30 days to get back on track, and what role would a book or publication take in the process?

Everybody is a little bit different, but I like the service business. I think about the areas of my expertise, which are in the areas of writing, marketing, PR, and media. I would pick one of those areas, and I would begin a campaign to get in front of the right people who are interested in that area. I wouldn't choose all three of those areas. When I started Bestseller Publishing, we really just focused initially on the actual writing of the book, the ghostwriting, and taking people through that.

I'd probably pick the ghostwriting piece because you can get 20,000-plus dollars if you have a decent ghostwriter. You're hard pressed to find a ghostwriter for less than 25,000 bucks these days. Most people charge more than that. I'd probably pick that piece of it. I do the marketing, and all I need to do is to have $25,000 and one person. Right? So I'm going to use my marketing wiles and find that one person.

Now, what role would a book play? I'm not going to write a great book in 30 days, but I would get started with it. I would start writing the chapters to the book and repurpose that content for social media, emails, blog posts, things like that, which would help get attention for free, for people that are interested in those things. I wouldn't just give them a chapter. People don't care about a chapter, but if you write it in such a way that answers their questions or solves their problems, they do care.

I would start writing my book and use the content of the chapters that I'm writing to begin promoting to my market—my audience. That's where my leads would come from. I would lead that back to a sales call. That's great stuff. I've been talking to a lot of people, and the thing that stands out is the focus on a high-ticket item.

It's best if you can create a $47 course or something with the book. One high-ticket item. One good client, that's all it takes. If you are an expert at your thing and you really can help somebody else achieve it, and it's a high-value thing, then that's the formula. Just offer it to the right people, and someone is going to take you up on it.

You can reach Rob at bestsellerpublishing.org.

5

BE THE AGGREGATOR BY STEVE LARSEN

What is your business?

I am massively against the way I was taught marketing in college. There was a certain thing around entrepreneurship that I was taught that was very against what we actually do.

When I first sat down in my entrepreneurship classes, they said, "In this course, you're going to learn how to write a 15- to 30-page business plan and learn how to present it in front of a board of investors to try and get funding for the business. You're going to go build."

I didn't know any different. I couldn't wait to do it. I loved *Shark Tank*, and I was so psyched out of my mind for this stuff. So that's what we did. I spent tons of time researching this thing. I remember I made a really cool real estate plan. I started trying to get funding for this thing, by traditional routes. When I met Russell, I realized the power of what he was doing. He literally taught me not to do any of that.

Skip all that crap. There's this thing in the world called the J curve.

You're expected for a while to go into debt. This is what I'm actively fighting. I want to make a whole show around this.

The first celebration is when you actually get funded. It's so exciting. You get funded, and you're going to go into debt, but you got funded. That's so cool. The next celebration is hopefully within a year, when you're not losing any more money. You don't *lose* money anymore, but you're also not *making* any.

The next celebration they taught you to have was when you actually get above what you borrowed. Then things go awesome for a while, and you actually take your business to the stock market and sell it, bring it through IPO. That was the plan. This is the J curve. It's everywhere. Much of our marketing world doesn't know about that, but it is all over the place, and I am vehemently against it.

My fight is against the J curve. You don't need to do the J curve. If you how to build a simple lead funnel, you can get customers for free and keep all their business and make way more money. You start right out from the get-go. Maybe you don't make any money for a little bit, but then it's—bam!—all you.

The business world doesn't like the funnel world very much because we were actively shaking the foundations that most everyone else has been teaching. I was at an event two years ago, with an international group of investors, and they brought in startups to get funding from this audience at the events. One woman was starting a credit card processing company, and her big bragging point was how much money she had raised. That doesn't compute to me. She raised money. She hasn't made any money. It's not the same as putting cash in your pocket, but that's the mentality, I guess. I was taught to go first, build the business structure, focus all your time on who's going to be on the team, who is the support person, who is fulfillment, who is the engineer, who's this, who's this, who's this...

There's so much focus on the business structure that once it's funded, there's nothing except pure, dumb hope.

Before I was at ClickFunnels, I was a good funnel builder. I built funnels, and I did all this research, and—boom, cash starts coming in. Yet, I hadn't learned how to charge. Yes, I was still broke.

Once, I made a funnel that was so good, the boss called me two weeks later and told me to turn it off. Who wants to turn off their red? Sales are good; what's wrong with you?

He told me, "Steven, you're sucking out all the cash from my business. You're selling our physical products so fast—I'm taking all the money from the business and going and buying more products. I can't pay my people. You're going to kill my business."

Whoa. It was the first time in my life I ever realized a stark, monumental difference between a funnel and a business. What I learned how to build in school was a business, not a revenue arm or a funnel.

I had never considered that. Build the funnel; don't go funding the funnel. When that generates revenue, use the revenue from that. Don't take it as profit. Go build the business with that, and suddenly you're off to the races. It's such a better way, but it is actively against what is being taught in the business world.

What have been the key factors to your success and why?

I think it was something my dad instilled in me: It is totally cool to fail. Failure is kind of fake. I wouldn't be where I am without my having tried 34 times to get a business to work, which is what I counted.

The obstacle is the way. I'm the least likely success story. I was kicked out of college for getting straight F's. I was a 35-percent-body-fat kid with a double chin, working on a third, and I had a massive fear of speaking to people. Huge fear. I was broke. I was a joke. Everything that I am now is the exact opposite of those things, and it is not an accident. I had a few really key experiences—getting kicked out of college was a big one. I had to wait four years to get back in, so I graduated late in life from college.

In those four years, I learned how to learn. I came back in and almost got straight A's. It was crazy. In high school, I was really big, and, suddenly, I got sick of it. I lifted weights every day and lost 45 pounds.

It was podcasting, actually, that taught me how to speak. It was me hustling every day for about a year before I ever met Russell. And then even in the first year I was with him, I'd get up like crazy. All these things in your life that you think are disqualifying you are actually the things that make you attractive in the future. I call it living the hook. It's hard for people because it starts with being honest.

I got kicked out of college. I had no discipline. People would say, "Steven, you're not that dumb." I was saying back, "No, man, I'm dumb." People want to give it to you soft. "You're not that fat." No, kid, you're chunky monkey right now, okay? You're a big kid. You focus on that. You have to say what it is. People can't do that—since they don't know enough about themselves, they can't say that about themselves and still feel good.

My self-worth was not based on my body-fat percentage. I believe a key factor of success is that there's a lot of garbage I don't choose to talk about or publish that I'm still going through. It's given me hope in the springboard. I can overcome that. When I do, it's suddenly like, man, failure is not real. I love that.

I can teach cash-flow models until I'm blue in the face, and everyone can learn them until they're blue in the face. Executing them is totally different. Somebody starts to run into their character flaws, which is natural. Someone starts to run into their abilities. Someone starts to run into whether or not they feel confident in themselves. Those things keep people back. I was a pushover, and I just got sick of it one day and started learning how to own my opinions.

I am 31 now. I was 28 then. I was struggling with talking as a 28-year-old. It wasn't until episode 80 that I actually started sharing some opinions, but then I'll get adults that are older than me and they're like, I can't do this.

No, you're *choosing* not to.

You don't try to hit a bucket list of stuff in your life all at once. That'll kill you. It's so unmotivating to just choose one thing and be like, I'm going to lean into this. That is very challenging for people to do. It's way harder than doing an actual business. I believe the reason someone doesn't do the stuff we teach is because the individual looks at themselves and says, "I'm not good at that."

They have to say instead, "I'm not good at that, and that's okay, but it's not okay for me to stay here."

And that's a very hard conversation for someone to have, honestly.

What is an unusual habit you have as an entrepreneur, and how does it help you persevere?

I am a comedy junkie. It's one of the easiest ways I cope. Even throughout the day while working, in the evenings, that tends to be the thing I turn to.

Also—this is going to sound weird, but I keep note of all the negativity that is being thrown at me and my own negative thoughts on top of it. I have a permanent marker and a punching bag in the shape of a guy. I write on the punching bag mannequin—it is one of those punching

Bobs or whatever—all the negativity. "One-hit wonder," "Russell's shadow." These are real things I hear from people.

Across the top of the mannequin covered in these black words is "Forgive and grow" in blue. It's big therapy for me for some reason. There's been times where I freaking cried in front of that thing. The point isn't to be a tank. Feel the emotion, then, after a while, sit back and say, "What am I going to do about it?"

I go in and feel. I listen to crazy rock music and stuff. It is part of the game. Part of the journey. I feel to the full extent.

And then I beat the crap out of it.

I have taken skin off my hands. Keep it simple, or you won't do it. Boom. I run at it like my life depended on it. It's one of the most freeing things. I never would have expected entrepreneurship to be a side education in self-development.

I don't know. It's working. It seems like it is.

If you lost everything—your book, your list, your products, your platform, your fame—and nobody knew who you were, what would you do in the next 30 days to get back on track, and what role would a book or publication take in the process?

I would immediately follow the money. I do this capitalist pig thing because I know I can be a smart marketer and try to ride the noise that's already there. It takes a lifetime to build momentum.

I would look to see where the noise is and find where the money is also around that.

A lot of old-school copywriting courses say you need to go and educate the public on their problem so your solution makes sense.

That's crazy, in my opinion. They already have the problem. They're consciously aware of the issue. When they see my message, my product easily slides. I would spend the first while trying to find where the large dollars are already being spent. What's something that's been there for a long time? That's one of the reasons I sell into that space, the click funnels.

I would focus very quickly. I would turn to podcasting and start bringing in big influencers who represent whatever market I'm going into, and I start pulling them on in. And, frankly, I probably do what you're doing right now and make a big book out of it, sell it, make a summit. A summit, selling info, products, or pulling influencers is easy—a drop in the hat, six-figure businesses. You're not going to do much; you're just the aggregator. That's the beauty of it.

I would find B- and C-level influencers, not the A's, because B's and C's want more of a platform, so they're willing to give and give and give and give. I would start crafting this hook. I've got a summit that we're working on right now. It is called Your Final Offer. If a doctor says you can't work in 90 days or you will die, you've got 90 days to set up that last offer. Suddenly, it makes them think. There's a lot of passion that has come from that—from these B- and C-level influencers.

You can visit Steve at stevejlarsen.com.

6

GIVE THEM THE OPPORTUNITY TO BUY YOUR ATTENTION BY NATHAN "ROCKY" ANDERSON

What is your business?

My primary business is online marketing, consulting, and building things for companies. The overarching theme of everything I've done has been digital real estate, as in building large numbers of niche websites and buying and selling. I started buying and selling web businesses back in 2000, when I was an SEO expert.

I would go out and look for websites that had a good sales process but had horrible rankings in the search engines. I'd buy them, fix them up, do the SEO on them, get them to the point where they're making good money, then turn around and sell them for 10 times what I bought them for.

This is bigger than it's ever been. Facebook is digital real estate; they're just so big that they can sell advertising on their platform alone. There's tons of websites out there that have huge amounts of traffic and use different advertising networks and different monetization schemes. A list of email addresses that you have permission to mail is a piece of real estate that's a digital asset you can buy and sell, or buy and sell access to. It's all a big game. People make huge amounts of money prospecting and speculating on domain names someone might want to buy. That's digital real estate.

If you're going to do something, do it right now. Don't think you'll do that later. If you find a domain name you want, register it. That's what I'm doing. Oh, it's just a horrible habit. I have 300-some domain names sitting in my account, not being used.

What have been the key factors to your success and why?

I think the key factors to most people's success in this business is a belief that you can. That's it. The core principle of just about anybody I know who has been successful in internet marketing is just believing that they're allowed to make millions, believing that they are good enough and they know enough to actually be a success. Just go for it and take action to the point of conclusion. It's really a belief. It's a belief you can do it. For me and Frank and a lot of other guys like him, it's being able to actually produce a book. The book is always the leading edge of a marketing effort.

It doesn't have to be an amazing book. You just want to have the ability to get people's attention and have them take you seriously. I sold an ebook when self-publishing was brand new in 2005. I did art at a content site, and this was an ebook. I purposely designed some to be press printed so I could have them with me and hand them to people. They'd say, "He's an author. He actually has a book." People talk about it being the best business card you can have.

That book was all of what, 68 pages? But they're just loaded with the best stuff he can come up with to give you an actionable format to have success with the information he gives you. Immediately, the law of reciprocity is in your favor. If you help people out, they feel obliged to help you back. They will always respect and trust you, so you can sell them all kinds of really expensive stuff.

I've made some horrible choices. I've taken on business partners that I absolutely had no business bringing into my company. That's going to happen, but after that happens, you're going to be at a point where you believe you can't anymore. You have to just take yourself up and dust yourself off and realize that you did make that million, and you can go back and do it again.

I've definitely had times when I thought I couldn't.

What is an unusual habit you have as an entrepreneur, and how does it help you persevere?

I don't smoke cigars anymore. That *was* my unusual habit, and I think that actually was very beneficial to being an entrepreneur, because it forced you to stop, go outside, and sit—just not work for 45 minutes and think about the things you're doing. I think that is actually really good for entrepreneurs. When I had an actual nine-to-five job, I had a long commute. I thought that commute was really beneficial because I had to shut down and be quiet and let myself think.

Stopping and actually letting your mind find solutions is really beneficial. But I figured it probably wasn't healthy to smoke a cigar every day.

How have you used a book for your business?

It is very effective as the primary lead for getting people to know and trust you. I've done several. I'm working on one now called *Digital Real Estate Secrets*. I'm talking about all the things I was just covering a moment ago. If you can prove you can help somebody by actually helping them, then they're gonna know they can trust you and be far more likely to take you up on other offers. Books are a great way to get an opt-in.

How do you make money from your books? How do you ensure this will continue to happen?

My goal is to not lose money on the book itself. Generally, I've done a lot of different formats for that. I've done a free digital version or an ebook they can download if they opt in to my list. I've found that kind of marketing isn't as effective as it used to be. It still works, but the trip-wire method of selling a book is much more effective these days.

The trip-wire method means you sell the book for a very low price, but you actually do charge people for it. Once you make somebody actually give you a credit card or PayPal or whatever, you've entered a different level of trust. At that point, you have the opportunity to upsell them into all kinds of other stuff.

It's extremely difficult to spend money on advertising and have it be profitable. You really do need to use it as a leader to a lot of your other programs. And you can. Authors do it all the time. It's just a very difficult thing to do. I like easy better. I like adding upsells to the point where it's easy to be profitable as well.

What bad advice do you often hear on the subject of authorship or writing a book for your business?

Don't make the mistake that a lot of people make and follow more than one method at the same time.

Don't think you can take someone's advice about a fiction book and apply it to nonfiction and have it work the same, or use half of someone's method and half of somebody else's. If you're not an expert, don't be putting stuff together like that. Follow one person's plan all the way from start to finish. They don't work together, oftentimes. You can choose to do that after you've made your first million.

If you lost everything—your book, your list, your products, your platform, your fame—and nobody knew who you were, what would you do in the next 30 days to get back on track, and what role would a book or publication take in the process?

I would pull from my knowledge and bang out a book as fast as possible, bang out a training—a video training course, a membership site. I like membership sites and continuity. Then I would use Facebook advertising to test and tweak and get people to take me up on that. You can't really do that with zero money. You do need some time and advertising revenue or investment to make that kind of thing work.

I'd say that the winning model is the book, a training that goes over what's in the book, and a continuity program of some type (a membership site where you keep getting paid).

That would be a book funnel. The way they used to do it, it was like you buy the hard copy, and if you wanted the digital version, you had to pay extra. I like to put the digital on the front. A trip wire works so much better. If you have another package—an all-inclusive type of package—that's always a good final upsell; a very expensive package.

It's funny, you never know who you have on the line. There are people who will drop $1,000 without even thinking about it. If they like what you've done, and they want the most of you they can get, you should let them. If you have a consulting package for $5,000 or $10,000, put it out there. I mean, there's nothing wrong with offering people something.

And if you're offering people your personal attention, then it should be expensive. Give them the opportunity to buy your attention.

You can reach Rocky at mixedsynergy.com.

7

GET BEYOND THE FEAR OF LIMITING BELIEFS BY SCOTT ANTHONY

What is your business?

No Excuse Life is my brand-new program all about helping people get beyond the fear of limiting beliefs that hold them back. Whether it is weight loss, relationships, business, or their comfort zones, people across all walks of life and income levels have hidden fears and obstacles. We also all have goals, dreams, visions, and things we want to do both in our personal and business lives. We constantly make excuses as to why we can't do it. I love to help people rip off what I call the BS layer—the "bull shift" layer—because we have to make an adjustment.

When we start getting out of the way and making a shift from the BS we keep telling ourselves, everything can start to open up. I love working with people who realize they have been the very problem themselves. We rewrite our next chapters. There is nothing better than getting past our own BS. It is wonderful when they realize they are only just one decision away.

We have to take action. It is so possible. I love to show people how!

What have been the key factors to your success and why?

Last night, I was in my son's school for a careers advisement event. They were telling my kids what subjects they should be choosing to set themselves up for college or for the careers they want to have. I was shaking my head at the crap these people were saying.

This is the same school that told me at 15 years old, "You're an imbecile. You will never amount to anything. Get used to having an average life."

I sat there thinking you are still peddling this to our kids because you have no knowledge or understanding of the entrepreneurial world.

I said to my son, "They are going to teach you to go to college or university. They're going to tell you that this is what you need to do."

But they won't know the statistics. Only 28 percent of people who go to college or university will ever use their degree. They are setting our kids up for a trajectory of ignorance. The world has changed. This school kicked me out at 15. We've all got triumphs, and we've all got struggles. Let me tell you my story.

Put your helmet on, because some people will get offended by this. The problem in most people's lives is they sit on the couch and watch *Game of Thrones* but won't do anything about changing their own circumstances. It's totally your responsibility. Everything that happened to me built a new muscle and was completely my responsibility.

I realized my future—and anybody's future—depended on how long we sat on the couch and which excuses we made. That's going to set the tone for the successes that we have.

We can justify it. We can say we've got school fees, the mortgage, electricity, and food. But those are all just excuses. If I lost everything today, I could walk away from everything, and if I still had my wife and four kids, I'd be the richest man in the world. What I would then do about it is entirely up to me.

Some people would just sit around and say, I need to watch Netflix. Other people would read a book; other people would buy a course; and 93 percent wouldn't do anything else other than that. They wouldn't implement what they had learned. It is the speed of implementation that is critical. Most people make friends with Netflix. And that's why they complain they haven't gotten what they want.

Is it tough love? Yes, but they're all just excuses. When I started out, I had to realize the excuses I've made so far have got me to where I was. Everything I get, everything I create—both the good and the bad —is my fault. When we personally take that on, we can change anything.

What is an unusual habit you have as an entrepreneur, and how does it help you persevere?

I find someone that is struggling with something, and I'll send them a message. I've got value. I like to sit and wait for them to like my comment. I'll give 10 people comments of empowerment: *I see you. You are noticed. You are valuable. You're making progress.*

And what happens is this makes me feel good because I'm *giving* to other people. I could just be selfish and say, "I'm having a hard time. It is not fair. The world is against me. Nobody understands me." I tried all that for years, and it did not actually give me anything.

When I started giving other people encouragement, belief, support, and sharing things with them, *that* worked for me. People were actually grateful. They appreciated it, and it made them feel good, which is a very unselfish act because it is a two-way street.

I will record a video for either myself to watch or for other people who are going through the exact same rut. I will say, "This is all a feeling. Here is what I found. Here is how we are going to get out of it." So I take my personal experience and share it, knowing that in five or 10 years, or next Thursday, someone is going to come across that video and it will actually help them. I call it paying it forward.

Don't go through anything alone. Lift someone else up and you get help, too. That is how I do things. A bit weird, perhaps, but it works.

How have you used a book for your business?

Yes, and when you see parts of your own story on a page and the power it has to transform other people's lives, it is an incredibly humbling and exciting moment in time.

The power of the written word and the sharing of yours and other people's experiences to help people learn from your journey is simply a powerful tool that works 24/7 to spread your message around the globe and help other people change their lives.

The best way of using a book in your business is not trying to get it as a money-making venture, but instead as a credibility platform. You get to say, "Read it at your own pace. Read it at your own leisure."

My life keeps changing. The things I've gone through, the stories—it's too long for a book. If we break it down into bite-sized pieces, people are able to finish it and extract one nugget. If you keep it really, really simple, people will love it. Then they're more likely to want to read something else.

That's the absolute key. Everyone is so busy buying books, buying courses, buying programs. Even if they manage to read the books from beginning to end, it's the implementation that holds people back. How do you get someone to take action? It's really simple.

If you make things simple for people, they are going to enjoy engaging with you.

If you lost everything—your book, your list, your products, your platform, your fame—and nobody knew who you were, what would you do in the next 30 days to get back on track, and what role would a book or publication take in the process?

Easy. If I lost everything, I would write a book titled *How I Lost Everything and How I'll Get it Back in 30 Days*.

Now, I may not have everything that I've got so far in 30 days, but it's about the mindset. I believe the lessons we go through enable us to learn and multiply the growth and speed of implementation. We can actually apply that in a week or a month. We don't have to relearn it. We already know they might have taken away our physical assets, but what we know mentally and emotionally, we can implement.

I would write the excuses that led to my demise and what I did about it. You can sell that to so many people.

Part of me wishes I lost everything for this very reason. It's a strange way of looking at things, but every time I've almost lost it, I've come back better, bigger, faster, stronger. Kids are looking at me. People are looking at me. That fuels me. When you write down your experiences, other people who are going through things 10 times worse will read it and find help in it.

I'll tell ya, I would love that challenge of losing everything, just to show people what can be done. Don't believe me? Try it and see what happens.

~

You can reach Scott at noexcuselife.com.

8

CONSISTENCY AND ATTENTION TO DETAIL
BY BRIAN BERNI

What is your business?

Book marketing.

What have been the key factors to your success and why?

The main factors that have played a fundamental role in my success have been consistency and attention to detail. Running ads for best-selling authors requires many different qualities, but being consistent, committed, and super attentive to even the slightest details is paramount.

What is an unusual habit you have as an entrepreneur, and how does it help you persevere?

It's more like a 'ritual' rather than a habit. I always keep track of everything I do. At this point, we run ads for hundreds of authors, so having some sort of logbook of the changes and tweaks we make is absolutely essential. I have what I call an 'ad journal' in which I jot down all the mods I make to specific campaigns together with my thoughts and ideas on how to improve the ads themselves. This small but effective 'ritual' helps me stay on track and focused on my job.

How have you used a book for your business?

Books are the lifeblood of my business! As an author myself, I know how big of an impact a book can have on a career. Take my short book on finding Amazon ad keywords, for example. It has been downloaded thousands of times, and it has landed me deals with some of my best clients. But most of all, it has helped authors take their businesses to the next level through the power of paid advertising.

What bad advice do you often hear on the subject of authorship or writing a book for your business?

I always tend to steer clear of those who promise stuff like "Write a book in a month and quit your day job," or "Become a best-selling author in 90 days." Sure, these feats can be achieved, but as someone who has an obsessive attention to detail, I prefer to focus on content rather than fast results. You may not write a book in a week, but you will write a *good* book, which is, and always will be, an asset for you and your business. And your audience will thank you for that.

If you lost everything—your book, your list, your products, your platform, your fame—and nobody knew who you were, what would you do in the next 30 days to get back on track, and what role would a book or publication take in the process?

First of all, I would find out where my target audience hangs out. It can be Facebook groups, forums, or other community-based platforms. I would then focus 100 percent on helping those people by answering their questions and essentially serving them to the best of my ability.

Being helpful and helping people is a natural 'authority-builder.' By being seen as someone who solves problems, you are instantly also viewed as an authority figure in your field. I would then make a list of the biggest and most recurring struggles my target audience has, and I would compile my answers in a book—a sort of 'Ultimate Guide to X.' There is no better way to build authority (and an audience) than to write a book on the subject. The next step would be to grow an email list of people who are interested in my topic.

My book would be essential in this step of the process, too. I could offer it for free as a 'reader-magnet,' which, in turn, would help me to find more and more readers. It's like building an ecosystem that functions on its own and revolves around the book you write. You help people through a book, and the very same people help you with figuring out what to write about.

You can reach Brian at BookAds.co.

9

WRITE A GREAT BOOK BY MATT STONE

What is your business?

I have many sites and small businesses, but my primary focus, since early 2018, has been 100 Covers. 100 Covers is a book cover design firm. We've successfully undercut the other book cover design providers in the industry without sacrificing quality, and we're growing at a berserk rate even though we've done next to no marketing and still only get a pathetic little trickle of traffic. I can only imagine how we'll be doing when someone actually finds our site!

What have been the key factors to your success and why?

In 2017, I launched an advertising service for authors, and, as is the nature of advertising, nearly *all* of the clients failed to see significant returns on their campaigns. While the business grew from nothing to over $20,000 per month in revenue, the whole thing collapsed just a few months later as the bad reviews started spreading around the publishing world in various groups and forums. It was a truly excruciating experience. We were *selling* what people wanted, but we couldn't *deliver* what they wanted. The whole business was mostly about trying to smooth over rocky client relationships. Pure misery!

With my head still throbbing from that miserable experience, I started 100 Covers with a completely new focus and attitude. I wanted to create amazing jobs for the workers and keep every single client happy. So I focused on helping the designers I hired to get good at their craft with unprecedented support and positivity. In no time, they went from inexperienced designers to truly competent professionals boasting about how they had found their "dream job."

And with the rise in quality of the work—while keeping prices low— our business has grown organically in tandem. We now exceed nearly *every* client's expectations, and on the rare occasion when a client is at first unsatisfied with their order, we go the extra mile to change their minds. We've given one refund this year, and even that client is having us do the rest of her series!

What business grows by a factor of 20 in 15 months without marketing? A *really* good one that's making people extraordinarily happy. Happy team + happy clients = a super easy business to build—and built to last.

What is an unusual habit you have as an entrepreneur, and how does it help you persevere?

I don't have many unusual habits really, but I do have an unusual circumstance. I overworked myself in 2014 trying to build three businesses at the same time, and I've never fully recovered. I can only work about 15 hours a week without re-aggravating my burnout condition. So I've had to figure out how to build and lead successful teams to do all the work, while I work extremely efficiently. It's forced me to figure out how to do what I think *everyone* wants to know how to do: make a living without working very much. I was terrible at it at first and nearly killed off my business completely. But I built it back from the ashes into something that is truly working now, and the future is bright!

How have you used a book for your business?

I haven't used a book for my current primary business yet, but I've used it in the past with great results. I've seen others do it, too— executing the book-business combo to absolute perfection. I do hope to write a book in the next year or two outlining my "lead a team" strategy that is working so well and use that to drive leads to my done-for-you business-building service. The only thing stopping me from doing it now is fear of it working too well! I'm not set up to handle clients for this service in bulk yet. It would kill me!

How do you make money from your books? How do you ensure this will continue to happen?

Honestly, I make money from the past success of my books and the reputation it built for me more than I'm making money from my books right now. I wrote books that, unfortunately, weren't my best effort. I was trying to just "write, publish, repeat" as we all were back in 2013 when that seemed to be the winning strategy. Well, reviews eventually killed off my best successes. When I publish my next book, it will be well thought out, done professionally in every way possible, and launched properly with at least six months of pre-launch dedication. It will work. That strategy always does.

What bad advice do you often hear on the subject of authorship or writing a book for your business?

I think publishing a book for your business *is* bad advice. You shouldn't publish a book as bait for something else. Sure, you should have something else lying in wait for those who read your book, love it, and want more, but books are sacred products and should be treated as such. Write a great book, and it will build your business for you. Write a book as marketing bait and watch an avalanche of reviews coming in saying that your book was just some big advertisement for other overpriced products and services!

If you lost everything—your book, your list, your products, your platform, your fame—and nobody knew who you were, what would you do in the next 30 days to get back on track, and what role would a book or publication take in the process?

I'd create a high-priced done-for-you service that makes a huge impact in people's lives and the best book I possibly could to go with it. This combination allows me to make a strong connection with readers as they sample my inexpensive product, and even just a handful of readers liking my work and trusting me to deliver more of the same in my "kitchen sink" product is enough to instantly start earning a livable income.

You can visit Matt at 100covers.com.

10

TRULY HELP SOMEONE BY EEVI JONES

What is your business?

I help people turn a magical spark of an idea into a fully-realized story that can inspire children's imaginations and boost their confidence. I do this for people who want to write books for two-year-olds all the way to middle-grade chapter books.

With the creation of my Children's Book University programs, I help aspiring children's book authors find incredible story ideas, and then assist them with the illustration process, publishing, and marketing. I do this with step-by-step video instructions that will showcase how I'm creating an entire book, so the student will see each step with an actual example that, in the end, will be published, so they'll see the complete launching process as well.

I have helped aspiring authors from all walks of life; from lawyers, neuroscientists, clinical psychologists, and filmmakers, all the way to moms, dads, and grandparents at all stages of their writing careers.

And with my Children's Book University, I am now able to help even more achieve their dreams of becoming children's book authors.

What have been the key factors to your success and why?

I always create external accountability whenever I work on something. I'm so very driven by external influences. And that's really best explained by Gretchen Rubin's book, *The Four Tendencies*. I'm a Obliger, which means I'm driven by outer expectations. What helps me achieve my goals and helps me create success is to create an external accountability system, be it a Facebook post announcing I will do this or that by a certain date, or joining a mastermind that meets regularly online to discuss what we'll work on next and then deliver at a certain date. These are all things that help me stay focused and reach my goals.

What is an unusual habit you have as an entrepreneur, and how does it help you persevere?

I'm not afraid to fail. If I have an idea, I just go with it. For years, I was made to believe this was a bad or negative trait. Only now have I come to understand that the most successful entrepreneurs have failed many times. What sets them apart from others is the fact that they didn't let their failures stop them and that they never gave up. Achievers see mistakes as a lesson; failures are simply stepping stones toward success.

How have you used a book for your business?

My book, *How To Self-Publish A Children's Book,* outlines the precise path to fulfilling an aspiring author's dream of becoming a published children's book author. Within this book, readers find everything they need to know to write, illustrate, publish, and market their paperback and ebook. With it, I created an exact blueprint to accomplish just that. And I truly held nothing back!

This book has been one of my biggest lead generators for my business. People who opt in via my lead magnet in my book are by far my hottest prospects. Eighty percent of my students purchased my book before they learned about and joined my programs and/or one of my one-on-one sessions.

How do you make money from your books? How do you ensure this will continue to happen?

My book, *How To Self-Publish A Children's Book,* has been a huge factor in quickly building trust and rapport with my clients and students. My book is essentially the marketing tool for my business that pays for itself. And no facebook or any other social media ad can beat that.

The way I ensure this will continue to be my number-one lead generator is by having created a lead magnet within the book that is truly relevant to the reader.

Once readers have entered my funnel, they are introduced to my courses and one-on-one coaching sessions.

I continuously add to my suite of courses. My inspiration comes directly from my subscribers. Whenever I realize that I'm answering the same question more than five times, I get straight to work and create an offer that addresses this particular need.

This helps me remain relevant to my readers, students, and clients, no matter where they are in their book-creation process.

What bad advice do you often hear on the subject of authorship or writing a book for your business?

I attribute the success of my book to the fact that I gave it my all. I didn't hold back.

Many who are writing a book for their business are so afraid that if they give it all away, there will be nothing left to teach. But this couldn't be further from the truth. There will *always* be more.

I get so many emails every single day. People won't run out of questions; and if you know your stuff, you won't run out of answers.

People will know whether or not you are holding back. They can tell if you're truly trying to help them get from A to B, or if you've simply written a few pages in order to lure them to your website.

If you provide true value, readers will want to be on your list. They will want to hear from you. They will want to read your emails whenever you're sending one their way.

Realizing that being true to myself and wanting to genuinely help others in any way I possibly can has been the biggest game changer for me and my business.

If you lost everything—your book, your list, your products, your platform, your fame—and nobody knew who you were, what would you do in the next 30 days to get back on track, and what role would a book or publication take in the process?

Day 1

A book would be front and center in my 30-day plan to getting back on track. I would start writing a "how-to" book, similar to my current *How To Self-Publish A Children's Book*. My book has been my biggest lead generator; not just in terms of numbers, but in terms of lead quality. People who purchase my book already know they want to write a children's book. They are extremely 'hot' leads.

Leads coming in from ads, on the other hand, may have had their interest piqued, but need a lot more time to warm up to me and my products.

Days 2–7

I'm giving myself about seven days to write this in-depth, step-by-step book. And as I'm writing my book, I will simultaneously create my opt-in as well. Instead of thinking of and creating my opt-in at the end, as more or less an afterthought, I will weave it throughout my entire book.

My opt-in *has* to be relevant to the readers of my book. It is my goal to have a close to 100 percent opt-in rate, which is absolutely doable with a highly relevant lead magnet. This will help me grow my email list quickly.

I will make sure to weave it into each and every chapter or section of my book, and will mention and reference it often, so it will become absolutely indispensable to the reader.

My opt-in is no longer a simple or nice-to-have freebie. Instead, it is a must-have—an important piece—that is completely integrated in the process described in the book. In order to accomplish what the reader has set out to accomplish when they first purchased the book, they will *have* to download this lead magnet.

During these first seven days, I will also schedule one of my editors so she is ready to work on my book right after I submit my manuscript to her on Day 7.

Day 8

As soon as my book is with my editor, I have my book cover designed. Before contacting my cover designer, I head over to Amazon to get some ideas by looking at books in my niche that are selling well.

This will help me greatly once I'm outlining what exactly it is I'm looking for with my own cover.

Day 9

I go ahead and sign up for a CRM (customer relationship management) system. I choose Kartra, because it will later also serve as my host for my courses I'm going to offer.

I create a landing page, and use Mediamodifier.com to create all the mockups of my offers. Alternatively, I could also have someone create these mockups for me on platforms such as Fiverr.com.

Day 10

On Day 10, I finish up my opt-in and upload all the templates, swipe files, and scripts I've created onto the download page.

Day 11

I write my script for my upsell video. If I still have time, I go ahead and record this short video using my iPhone. Once completed, I upload it onto my Kartra page.

Day 12

Today, I'm dedicating the entire day to finding and joining relevant Facebook groups and starting to interact with the groups' members.

Interacting with the members is something I will want to do for at least 20 minutes a day from this day forward. This will be my daily social media homework. Connecting with these people now will help me out big time once I'm ready to launch my book and offer my products and services.

It is in these groups where I'll learn what people in my niche really need help with, which will be really useful once I start creating my individual offers. And I'm putting myself directly onto their radar by actively supporting them and answering their questions, which, in turn, helps to build trust and rapport quickly.

Day 13–15

I start creating some sort of mini-course or masterclass. This will be my upsell for anyone who is about to download my templates, swipe files, and scripts.

Just like with the original lead magnet, I will have to make sure the upsell I'm offering is the next logical step for the person who just purchased my book.

This concludes the first half of this expedited journey of reinventing myself.

Day 16

On Day 16, I write the script for my three-to-five-part email sequence. This will be automatically sent out to people who didn't purchase my upsell offer the first time around. The purpose of these emails is to remind them of the offer.

Day 17

I finish building my funnel by uploading the email scripts I've created the previous day.

Day 18

Using my favorite social media channel(s), I finally get to share what I have created and worked on these past couple weeks. I start assembling a launch team for my book to ensure a good number of initial downloads and reviews once my book launches.

Day 19

By now, I should have received my manuscript back from my editor. I will dedicate the entire day to working on the suggestions and changes made by my editor.

Day 20

My cover design should be finished and finalized by now, so I will spend the day assembling and formatting my book.

Day 21

Today, I have two main tasks. First, I'm going to send out my edited and formatted book to my launch team members. I do this today so they have ample time to take a look so they can prepare a short one-to-two-sentence review that can be uploaded as soon as my book goes live.

The second task of the day is to reach out and secure some podcast interviews or guest-blogging opportunities. I approach blogs and podcasts that cater to my target audience and formulate my pitch in such a way that my guest appearance (be it on podcasts or in articles) would be a win for the host, his or her listeners or readers, and myself.

Having previously been featured in places like *Forbes*, *The Creative Penn*, and *Kindlepreneur*, I know that if the needs and interests of all three are aligned, securing such a guest appearance will be fairly easy and straightforward.

To see how exactly I go about approaching different influencers in my niche to successfully pitch an article or request an interview, check out my free three-part Influencer Outreach mastercourse right here:

http://www.eevijones.com/freecourse/

Day 22–24

It's time to create my main course. This shouldn't be too hard, since I already have an in-depth outline for it—my book. I will take the next three days to create and edit the videos.

Day 25

Today is set aside to write the sales copy for the course. Ideally, I'll also create a short video that will go over the main benefits and features of the course.

Day 26

More copywriting! Only people who went through my very first email and upsell sequence will get to this point. I will now have to write my second email sequence that will introduce my main course.

This second sequence will again consist of about three-to-five-part emails. This will be automatically sent out one to two weeks after the lead went through my first email sequence. By now, people either already started reading my book or went through my mini-course they purchased as an upsell. They have gotten to know me better just by completing my first email sequence, and are now ready to be intro-duced to my flagship program.

The timing will be perfect, because it will take a while for my guest posts and podcast interviews to go live, once the articles have been submitted and the interviews have been recorded.

Day 27

I reserve this entire day to prepare for my podcast interviews and write the articles for my accepted pitches.

I will make sure to listen to at least one or two episodes of each podcast I'm invited to in order to get a feel for the host and his or her interview style.

I will also read one or two blog posts of all the websites I'm about to write articles for. This will help me greatly in determining and emulating the voice that particular blog is written in.

Day 28

Today is the big day! It's time to officially launch my book. This is where all pieces will fall into place. The complete back end has been completed and set up for this moment.

I will share my launch on all my private social media accounts, as well as in the Facebook groups that I joined on Day 12, provided this sort of promotion is allowed.

Today is also the day I ask my launch team members to post their prepared reviews on Amazon.

Day 29

My book has been launched and should already have between five and 10 book reviews thanks to my launch team. Getting my book in front of as many potential buyers is key. It's time to set up some Amazon ads for my book. For this, I'm going to use some of the money I previously generated with my upsells.

Later on, once the book and funnel have generated more sales, I can broaden my marketing efforts by creating Facebook ads as well. The ads will lead to either my book or directly to the course I created.

Day 30

This is the very last day of this 30-day plan. Today, I'll be sure to do two things:

First, I will follow up with all launch team members who have not yet left a review. As the saying goes, the fortune is in the follow-up. So I'll make sure to reach out to each member individually, letting them know how much they are appreciated and how grateful I am for their time and support.

And the second thing I'll make sure to do today is…rest! It's important to take a moment to look back and appreciate all that I've done these past 30 days. This was an intense month, but it will pay off big time, as all these created assets are now running on autopilot and are truly evergreen.

Final Thoughts:

While writing a book may seem daunting and overwhelming at first, it's important to remind myself that it's simply a record of my knowledge in a very specific field that I already know more about than most people out there. I know that with the writing of this book, I'll be able to help so many others to navigate through the children's book creation process that took me months (if not years) to master on my own.

So in moments where you simply want to quit and give up, let the knowledge that you're truly helping someone out there be what guides you. Here's to an amazing 30 days!

You can reach Eevi at eevijones.com.

11

THE OPPORTUNITY TO TRY SOMETHING NEW BY RICHARD MCCARTNEY

What is your business?

KBookPromotions.com

What have been the key factors to your success and why?

In today's Internet age, it helps to be tech savvy, and with a background in eCommerce, this came naturally to me.

Combine this with an entrepreneurial spirit driving me to reach a certain goal (and mine was to create a business helping self-publishing authors to find new readers) and you have some of the key factors you ask about.

However, without a "why" this would not be enough. I started by promoting my father's books, which had previously been reasonably successful. I was lucky enough to be promoting this back in 2015 during the gold-rush years when promoting ebooks on self-publishing was less competitive, Amazon was still a bit wet behind the ears, and everyone was still figuring out the best ways to promote ebooks. Then came big changes such as Kindle Unlimited, Facebook Ads, Amazon Ads, BookBub Featured Deals, you name it. I was one of the few testing things out with a group of fellow authors, often breaking with conventions to promote our books.

During this time I found my "why" for doing all this: finding and building a community of like-minded authors and readers willing to help and share experiences to discover what promotional methods worked and which did not.

From this experience, I wrote my own books on self-publishing, sharing with the outside world how Amazon really works in promoting books and how authors could best leverage this. Most of these acquaintances and connections I made along the way developed into longtime industry friendships—people I could trust and rely on. These people continue to be my "why"—the driving force for continuing what I do today, with the goal of creating a trustworthy, reliable network for readers.

What is an unusual habit you have as an entrepreneur, and how does it help you persevere?

I can touch my elbow with my nose. You try it! It's a very unusual habit that few can achieve.

Actually, no. I'm only kidding. I think that's actually impossible. One of my real unusual habits is always playing tricks, often silly magic tricks with the readers and authors I work with. You can find some of these in my books. I have to admit it's a great way to let off some steam and remain sane during the endless hours answering emails, phone calls, or video-conferences. As the old saying goes, "You don't have to be mad to work here, but it helps."

How have you used a book for your business?

Most of the books I have published include a suggestion to try out my book-marketing services.

I recently converted one of them into an audiobook, and the very next day I got an email from an author saying she listened to it and would like to work with me in promoting her book. Books can be used as a business card to help find new customers.

How do you make money from your books? How do you ensure this will continue to happen?

While I do okay from the sales of my books, their main purpose is twofold. The first is to share experiences and best practices in what works and does not work in trying to promote your book. Secondly, it's to introduce my book marketing services. I think it's no secret that many nonfiction books today make more money from the back-end services they offer, and I am no exception to this.

Given that I have a customer base in the thousands with a customer return rate of about 65 percent, I am confident that the money I make from my book and my business will remain healthy for a good number of years, but nobody can be complacent. The market changes, and so must I. This is why I plan to expand the number of books I write and the services I provide to authors, including the promotion of audiobooks and PR services that get authors into the top press sites in the U.S.A.

What bad advice do you often hear on the subject of authorship or writing a book for your business?

I cover this in the first chapters of my book, *Self-Publishing: The Secret Guide To Becoming A Best Seller*, and, boy, there really is a lot of bad advice out there. As my expertise is more in marketing books than writing them, I would have to say that one of my biggest pet peeves is the belief created by many that social media alone will help you reach hundreds, if not thousands, of new readers.

Heed my words: beware of using social media—or better said, beware of investing a lot of time on social media. Sports stars use it, politicians use it, journalists use it, kids use it, the neighbor's cat probably uses social media. Everyone uses it!

Don't get me wrong. Facebook and Twitter might be great for sharing news and pictures and for getting updates from others on what is going on. But it's also great for getting lots of trashy information, such as what a certain celebrity ate for dinner. While social media does have some value, it is rarely of any use at all for converting social media visitors to buyers of your book.

If you don't believe me, please refer to the statistical evidence I provide in my book based on many tests carried out these last several years.

The other deception I see comes from those who provide tools that tell you how many sales you can make for your book based on the Amazon sales of other books in similar categories. They will show a book in a certain category reaching an Amazon sales rank of #1,450 and determine they are selling 50 books a day at $2.99. They then calculate how much money you would make each month based on this number. What they don't tell you is that no book has a steady Amazon sales rank. The ranking changes every hour on Amazon, so a book's sales ranking can vary from #1,450 to #222,900 in a day—and you won't get many sales if your sales rank is at #222,900. So be careful with promises you hear from unsolicited sources. It is best to rely on authors or other promoters you have worked with to provide reliable information.

If you lost everything—your book, your list, your products, your platform, your fame—and nobody knew who you were, what would you do in the next 30 days to get back on track, and what role would a book or publication take in the process?

Hey, Rome was not built in a day. I think we are kidding ourselves to think we can rebuild where we were if we lost everything. Success takes time. There is no magic solution that can get us running at full speed again in such a short period of time. I would either find a nice spot in the sun where I could sip piña coladas to drown my sorrows, or use it as time off to recollect my thoughts and perhaps consider something new to do.

PS: That's exactly how I started off in the self-publishing business. No, not after drowning myself in piña coladas, but in losing my previous job of 10 years and deciding to try something new. Life can be strange that way.

You can reach Richard at kbookpromotions.com.

12

PERSISTENCE PAYS BY CONNOR BOYACK

What is your business?

I'm a full-time freedom fighter. Eight years ago, I started a nonprofit to work on legal reforms in Utah. I saw a need for a voice of liberty in our state. Now we have about a dozen employees, changed dozens of laws, and had a bang-up job doing it. We've passed all sorts of first-in-the-nation laws on free-range parenting, lemonade stand for freedom, and getting rid of home-based business licenses, data privacy, all sorts of stuff. That's what I do full-time. How it led to books is kind of a fun story.

When my kids were little, I would come home and lack any language with which to talk to them about what I was doing all day. Like, how do you talk about property rights to a five-year-old? How do you help little kids understand justice, liberty, free markets?

I tried to find a book on how to talk about free markets to kids. There was nothing. That led to the idea of doing the Tuttle Twins books.

Each of the books in the Tuttle Twins series is based on an original book or essay from decades ago, centuries ago, that espouses and teaches these ideas. For example, take these classics, you know, like *Economics in One Lesson* by Henry Hazlitt, a very popular book, and *The Road to Serfdom* by F. A. Hayek. When you read these, the language they use—the style of English—is hard for people today, especially young people. So we basically take the core ideas from those books and wrap them in a fun story. Then, yeah, these are kids' books, but in reality, we're reaching a lot of parents as well who've never read those original books.

Our first book of the series was *The Tuttle Twins Learn about the Law*. When we saw this market opportunity, I approached a friend of mine, Elijah Stanfield. He also had young kids, so it clicked. He understood this opportunity and the need, and he became the illustrator. That first book was based on Frederic Bastiat's essay, "The Law," which is very brief but very powerful, written in 1850. For us both, that was an influential essay, and so we wanted to pay homage to that. We had struck a chord.

The first part of the process is refreshing my memory. A lot of these books I've read years ago as part of my own self-education. I'll go back and read through them, kind of pick apart these ideas. Then I try to find different, creative ways to come up with the story and which ideas can be taught. I don't have a magic bullet for that. I write the essay. Elijah gives a lot of input because he's very like-minded.

We'll come up with the rough draft, and then Elijah will get to work doing illustrations. It's a very collaborative process between he and I to come up with something. We're both giving one another feedback. We have some folks on our team, close friends, who will beta-read the rough drafts with their kids and help us out. We see what worked, what didn't work, and we can refine it to a good book before we hit publish.

Books, to me, are marketing assets. They are a fantastic way to reach audiences that I otherwise might not be able to reach. They're not on my email list. Maybe they'll never come to one of our events. Maybe they have no clue who I am, but a friend of a friend of a friend will recommend these books to their kids and their friends. Word of mouth marketing opportunities are substantial because when new people are introduced to the books, they learn about the ideas, which is our purpose. Then they're learning about who I am. They're following me online, they're connecting to our organization, they're buying other books. We see the books as a vehicle to more aggressively get the ideas out, rather than just posting on social media to people who already know who we are.

When you provide tangible value in the form of a book, you get a level of appreciation among your readers who not only value the purchase that they made, but have an intrinsic desire to want to share, especially among young families. Moms and dads who are friends with one another recommend books to their friends to read to their children. When you're offering that value to them, they're posting on Instagram about it. They're sharing in their church group or neighborhood. It's a great way for us to reach new audiences.

Once you have a book, you don't have to sell yourself anymore. You don't have to say, "Hey! I know what I'm talking about." You just say, "Hey! I've got a book you should read." The book tells the person you know what you're talking about.

What have been the key factors to your success and why?

One of my most motivating influences has been a simple acronym that my late grandfather would always say to me: PPPG. Persistence Pays Pretty Good. I recognize the wisdom of that silly little statement —so few people are persistent in the things they want. Something holds them back, whether it's laziness, feelings of inadequacy, or uncertainty. They stay within their lane rather than thinking outside the box. My grandfather and my parents instilled in me an understanding of the importance of persistence. This has given me the drive necessary to hustle, to stick with it when failures come. Persistence alone has helped me continue to commit to and explore new ideas.

PPPG has burned into my brain. I've internalized that, and I'm always trying to be persistent. I've written 17 books in a decade. I'm going to publish five more this year. The nice thing with persistence is that it's the principle of momentum. Once you gain momentum, it becomes a self-fulfilling cycle. It's easier to maintain momentum and increase it than to create it from a stop. I've figured out book publishing, I've figured out marketing, I've figured out e-commerce. Now that I know these things, I already know these things. I don't have to continually relearn them. I can go to the next thing.

What is an unusual habit you have as an entrepreneur, and how does it help you persevere?

I'm a very productive person, and there are two things I found come with that. The first is a level of sacrifice that comes when you're pulling 60- to 80-hour weeks trying to build a start-up. I've certainly seen that in my own life. My work is my hobby. People have hobbies, and it's a wonderful thing. I'm not knocking them. But I am so enthralled with what I do that if I have free time, I want to spend it doing "work." Because, for me, it's not work.

It's play.

I enjoy what I'm doing. I find fulfillment in it. And especially where it's a purpose- and passion-driven project, my work involves trying to improve other people's lives. It's service, and anyone who does community service knows that you gain personal benefit when you are influencing another person's life.

Through my work, whether it's education or changing laws to help other people, there definitely is that neurochemical response. The endorphins are running, the oxytocin, and the pleasure centers are being stimulated. Being able to find an opportunity in life where you love what you do is the magic bullet. Work isn't drudgery. It's not a means to an end. It is the end itself that I'm very much wrapped up in. I recognize there are people who have different paths where that's just not part of their life mission or opportunity, but for me personally, being able to love what I do means that I'm playing all day long and having a ball doing that.

How do you make money from your books How do you ensure this will continue to happen?

What I've actually found wisdom in is doing a series of books. There's something about having multiple books that creates a sense of legitimacy that a single book, in my experience, does not. When I published the third book in our series, things changed for us. Especially for children's books—kids love reading a whole series. Parents love buying the whole series for their kids to have the complete set.

I intentionally did not sell any of our books on Amazon. I set up our own funnel.

I wanted to know all my customers. We did the fulfillment ourselves. That came at a cost and a sacrifice, but it was worth it because I wanted to know my universe. I wanted to build my audience. When book number two came out, I wanted to know everyone who had bought book one so I could market to them rather than throwing it up on Amazon and hoping everyone who bought book one at some point would think, oh, I wonder if they've done another book. No—I want to directly market to all those people. I want to do email marketing, I'm going to do text marketing, I want to do snail-mail marketing, go after these people.

So we did it all on our website the first few years, and we put it on Amazon only once we had a good marketing engine up and running. Even to this day more than 95 percent of our sales are all through our website.

I wanted to master the entire self-publishing process to not only capture as much profit as possible but to also do paid advertising. If I had a publisher, my profit margin as an author would be basically close to nil.

Many publishers aren't doing effective or aggressive marketing themselves. Their budgets are going to zero. They key for me was internalizing the operation and controlling everything A to Z so we would just do it all ourselves. I'm doing all the marketing and fulfillment. We have our customer list, and that has now been gold. We have 80,000 families reading these books. I know who they all are with the exception of the few who are now buying on Amazon. Every time a new book comes out, I've now got my customer base who will ravenously purchase the new book and recommend it, and it grows and grows. The question of profit of the books has really become self-publishing and knowing who all your customers are.

To be a good author, you need to be a good marketer. It's irresponsible as an author not to understand how to market what you've slaved away at creating. Gone are the days when you can outsource that and think someone else is going to do it all for you. I think especially if you want profit, opportunity, maximum impact, and reach, you need to be thinking of yourself as a marketer.

What bad advice do you often hear on the subject of authorship or writing a book for your business?

What bad advice? That's a great question. No one's ever asked me that. I think it's easy to be gun shy as a new author, and to want to refine and refine and refine and edit over and over again before you get out the door. I'm a big fan of shipping the minimum viable product.

Don't take forever trying to write this masterpiece. If it's your first thing, ship it, put it online, publish chapter by chapter, and get feedback along the way. Plan on getting your first book out there. It may not be a huge hit, but you've now learned the process and it's set you up for the next book, which is going to be even better. Sales of your first book will improve when you get your second book out. Then people who learn about your second book want to go back and figure out what that other book that you did was. I think the bad advice, if I can call it that, is maybe more of an internal thing that authors sometimes feel and advise themselves. And that is that they have to have perfected a product. They have to get an agent, and they have to get a publisher.

No. The barriers to entry in this market are gone. It is very easy with just a few hours of work to learn how to self-publish and to do it at a quality level, with like 250 bucks. You can get a very professional design for your book that looks excellent and positions your book in a very professional manner to your audience. With minimum effort on Upwork, you can find someone to edit the book professionally for you.

There's just so many ways online to do it all yourself, to learn the process and do it more quickly, have more control over it, gain more profit from it. Bad advice is thinking that the publishing process of yesteryear is what new authors today have to resign themselves to.

There's so many other opportunities today to just ship that minimum viable product, make a name for yourself, build your portfolio, and keep writing and keep publishing.

If you lost everything—your book, your list, your products, your platform, your fame—and nobody knew who you were, what would you do in the next 30 days to get back on track, and what role would a book or publication take in the process?

What I would do is I would set up an online funnel and some paid ads to develop a warm audience. I would do an ebook, because that is far less friction. I want to get things going. I would spend a day producing an ebook specific to my audience. For me, it's freedom, free markets, and property rights. I would do some kind of behind-the-scenes tips and tricks and updates. I would write a simple ebook, build my email list, then set that up on automation for the next few weeks while I work on probably a booklet or something that's smaller and tangible that I can ship. Then I'd start doing some upselling to those people to be able to build some revenue off of it as well as with other related products that they'd be interested in.

My goal in having a passion-based business is I would want to establish myself with an authoritative voice within my community as someone who's trusted and should be listened to, whose ideas should be adopted. I would be using the email list I'm building from that ebook funnel, too. Do an automated series of emails that presents myself and my backstory to establish myself as a person of interest and a trusted person that they can listen to.

I'd probably start a Facebook group as an exclusive community for them as well so they can have access to me. Some of that takes a while, obviously, to manufacture or put together. I would then at least have a fertile ground with which to start planting. Because I've kind of cultivated them in those first 30 days, that would set me up for later success as I start producing some of the assets I know this new audience is going to benefit from and purchase.

For those interested in the books, check out my books featuring the Tuttle Twins. That's where we offer a bundle pack of the books. We offer free activity workbooks for each of the books as well. You can get the audio books, if that's more of interest to you. We target kids aged roughly five to 11.

13

A PURPOSE TO TRANSFORM YOUR LIFE BY JERÓNIMO CABRERA ROCHA

What is your business?

My business is to promote the growth of people and organizations to achieve their maximum expression.

To achieve that, we use methodologies for immediate implementation and high-impact that are a means to achieve that mission effectively:

- Conexo S.R.L.

We promote the growth of people and organizations to achieve their maximum expression, through Neuro Linguistic Programming (NLP) tools and whatever else is necessary. We help our clients avoid the pain of trial and error in their own experiences, and connect it with the pleasure of achieving their objectives through methodologies, tools, and techniques tested by the most successful minds on the planet.

- Consultora Optimiza

We help with practical, step-by-step guides for entrepreneurs to avoid stagnation or bankruptcy with proven methodologies of high-impact implementation and immediate results, which allow them to make their companies profitable in the short term.

- Apio verde Catering

We revitalize the energy of the people who lead their lives through meal plans.

- Action Group

We empower entrepreneurs to achieve their wildest dreams by providing excellent services to their clients in the field of real estate.

What have been the key factors to your success and why?

The most important success factor was **to recognize what I have come to do in this world.** I described my purpose or personal mission in an essay that would later transform my life.

In this process, I used all my intellect, emotion, and physical expression to reaffirm what my purpose is. I also experienced the weight of why it is important to define and visualize the transformation that would occur when starting to live from that place.

From that day on, I understood that efforts to increase talents, skills, and abilities would not have much weight without preparing myself psychologically with forcefulness and clarity.

It is said that before embarking on a trip you need to know the destination, and this statement of purpose raised the destiny of my efforts, constantly serving me to choose what to believe, how to feel, what to do, and decide, to align in that direction.

I want to emphasize that for years I focused my efforts on growing the business I started without realizing that this action only represented 1 percent of my progress. What really began to impact results was when I focused my efforts on improving my mentality—or as many call it, in the personal growth or development that I subsequently printed on myself.

This revolutionized my progress, stopping the frustration of years and turning that energy into goals achieved and the basis for achieving the results I get today. If you only model this experience that it took me 20 years to know, I guarantee you, dear reader, that this book will pay thousands of times its cost and will have positive repercussions throughout your life.

Without knowing anything about you, where you are from, what you do for a living, how you feel, what you think, who you are, or what your mission is, I assure you: if you do this small task with focus and enthusiasm, you can give a positive rudder in your life and your work, from which you and all the people you love and want to serve can benefit, which in this case is me for you.

Before presenting the following challenge, I want to express my gratitude to Robert Dilts, co-creator of Neuro Linguistic Programming, who personally taught me at the University of Santa Cruz California the impact of Neurological Levels and how to absorb the power of a purpose in a couple of weeks' training. From that day on, my life would never be the same, and it is my wish that it be so for those who continue reading.

CHALLENGE

(This challenge can begin to give you ideas of your purpose.)

Write the answer to this question on a notebook—preferably with yellow sheets and a red pen.

WHY DO YOU WANT TO BE WILDLY SUCCESSFUL IN LIFE?

Express it in one sentence. Yes, stop your reading. Get the paper and pen so you can write it right now, and do it as you can, but do it right now, remember that, if you do it with the expectation that it is perfect, it will be much harder for you to do it, and if you do the exercise as simply as you can, you will get the greatest possible benefit from this dynamic.

Take determined action!

If you are already with what is necessary, write the answer to that question.

Example:

I want to be wildly successful because in this way I can help the people around me: family, collaborators and friends.

Then answer question number two:

WHY IS IT IMPORTANT TO YOU (and write down the answer to question number one): _____?

Example:

"And why is it important for you to help the people around you, your family, collaborators, and friends?"

Sample response: *Because I will be happy to have served them and that connects me with a sense of well-being of doing the right thing.*

Now answer question number two, six more times:

"And why is it important for you to be happy, serve your environment and connect with the well-being of doing the right thing?"

Continue to answer that way a total of seven times, until you discover the deepest possible reason, perhaps not visible so far. That answer will become the engine and the wind that will blow your ship's sails, enhancing your strategies and mechanisms to reach your destination. The best thing is that it will be your destination.

If, in the process, you connect with emotions that come off, be aware that they are energy in motion and it is totally normal to have them when you respond with the heart. These answers will lead you to recognize the real reasons why you are present in this life and why you do many of the things you do.

There are thousands of ways to discover your purpose; this is just one of them. The important thing is that you have it so clear your business is designed to finance the trip.

Personally, I had the belief that I should choose between earning money or serving people. Today I am aware that thousands of people have managed to serve people and on the way have amassed fortunes. I want you to find a way to serve with passion through your current or future entrepreneurship, while in the process you receive all the money necessary to live as you wish.

In the process of your success you will have to make decisions about which projects to face and which to ignore. Next is a tool that supports me to decide which projects to engage in.

- Possible Project:

Implement fast food franchises

Impact in economic terms from 1 to 10: 7

Alignment of the project to my life / happiness purpose from 1 to 10: 1

Total rating from 1 to 10: 7 + 1 = 8

- Possible project:

Launch workshops and books on the internet that help entrepreneurs avoid stagnation or bankruptcy and connect them with proven methodologies that make their company profitable in the short term.

Impact in economic terms from 1 to 10: 9

Alignment of the project to my life / happiness purpose from 1 to 10: 10

Total rating from 1 to 10: 9 + 10 = 19

With this assessment, I choose the last project. This is a quick example of how to choose projects that, in addition to satisfying your personal purpose, serve your customers with excellence and consequently earns you money.

Once you have defined your purpose, I suggest you reformulate your identity and your beliefs. You can do this with a certified coach in Neuro Linguistic Programming (NLP). This will accelerate the effects. You can contact me to do it through a virtual platform or with any Certified Coach, preferably a specialist in discovering your Mission or Purpose, your definition of identity, and the change of beliefs.

This specialist must be very well trained. I strongly suggest coaches certified by Robert Dilts, because I am witness of the passion and dedication that is printed on the Neurolinguistic Programming University (NLPU). Every one of the coaches who receive that personalized and deep training learn this knowledge with all their mind and body.

What is an unusual habit you have as an entrepreneur and how does it help you persevere?

Place reminders publicly in the office and in the house that remind me about the importance of what I came to do to this world. This gives me strength, resources, strategies, ideas, and everything I need to persevere with strength and determination.

These reminders can be expressed in this way:

Daily habits, such as exercising while listening to encouraging music and repeating statements that remind me about my power and how to move on.

Thanking reminds me of how lucky I am, and from that state, I can persevere more easily.

Treasure maps or collages with images of what I want to achieve, lit in visible places that remind me of the objectives. This supports me to stay focused and therefore to persevere.

Affirmations or statements written in the present tense. They remind me who I am, what I believe, and why I must persevere.

How have you used a book for your business?

A book can help you in many ways in your business. It provides you with authority in your area of expertise, and it generates credibility in your brand during the process.

It gives you visibility and media coverage, making it easier for your audience to comment about you and the value you deliver with your work, facilitating how they find you in the market.

A book generates attention in supporting your marketing as a converter of attention in money. The more people know about your work, they more likely they are to request your services.

I am using books as a means to impact people through the tools and experience that I have learned and accumulated in the last 20 years as an entrepreneur, consultant, and coach. This purpose brings benefits in the marketing of my services.

In January 2019, during a training called Business Mastery held in Palm Beach, USA with thousands of entrepreneurs from more than 40 different nationalities, we brainstormed how to attract more leads (prospects interested in our service or product) to our business. When Tony Robbins, the coach who directed that program, asked the public some idea on how to get more prospects, I raised my hand, and without a doubt, my contribution was: write a book! Tony Robbins validated it as one of the ideas that remained as possible strategies for all the entrepreneurs who attended that event.

Writing a book puts you in a space where you can spread your value by serving people who may later work with you.

How do you make money from your books? How do you ensure this will continue to happen?

Writing places me as a reference. Delivering value in what I write positions me in the mind of the target audience as a closer relationship than they could choose to buy a product or service, because almost nobody buys from people or companies with whom they have no relationship.

To ensure that this continues, I will publish books where I will contribute years and years of experience of my own and others, in order to give value.

What bad advice do you often hear on the subject of authorship or writing a book for your business?

The most limiting tips related to making a book for my business that I have received are:

- Writing a book is something that takes a long time to learn.
- Writing a book is an activity that does not contribute to the growth of your business—it is a personal activity.

If you lost everything: your book, your list, your products, your platform, your fame and nobody knew who you were, what would you do in the next 30 days to get back on track, and what role would a book or publication take in the process?

I would identify a couple of communities and their needs. I would get experts who can contribute solutions for the members of those communities and invite them to write a book with all the solutions.

I would solvent the book with each of the contributions of the co-authors who will be able to expose their level of knowledge in them, and with this I would add a lot of value to the readers.

I would use the concepts of the book *Influence* by Robert Cialdini to launch these books to the market. I would sell them at irresistible prices, with subsidized shipping if necessary, so that many people can experience that level of content.

I would invite only those who finish the book to be part of an online mastermind on the subject, where they can expand their minds with all the experts. I would invite authors and position myself among these communities as an authority leading these groups of master-minds—which, in addition to creating a lot of value for the partici-pants, would give me back the lost income in just 30 days.

14

THE GROWTH MINDSET BY DEREK DOEPKER

What is your business?

I help people write, publish, and market best-selling books.

What have been the key factors to your success and why?

When I first started out as an entrepreneur, I was a dead-broke car valet and aspiring rockstar. I now realize that my background in music as well as my passion for health and fitness paved the way for success as an entrepreneur.

Growing up, my friends admired my ability to play guitar. They would say things like, "You're talented." But they never saw how terrible I was when I first started playing. It was through relentless practice that I became a master. This taught me that skills and talents are rarely hardwired. You can almost always develop skills through perseverance and training. A key factor to my success is having a growth mindset and dedication to mastery.

When I started writing music, I worried my songs would suck. And they did. At first. But I also realized no one had to hear my sucky songs. Music composition taught me it's okay to create crappy drafts and improve as you go. I could keep reworking songs until they were good enough to play for others.

Later in my life, when working with aspiring authors, I often see they slow themselves down because they want their writing to be great. Paradoxically, when you give yourself permission to do crappy work, you often end up with something much better over time. You shut off the critical part of your brain and give your creative side permission to run free.

A key factor in my success is giving myself permission to create crappy work and improve as I go.

When teaching guitar lessons, a new student came in who had been practicing on her own for months. As a result, she'd developed some bad habits we had to undo. Her hard work was actually sabotaging her success because she didn't get feedback. She didn't have outside eyes to see her blind spots. A key factor is getting quality feedback from an outsider.

Fitness showed me one workout, no matter how great, won't create lasting change in your body. As cliché as it is, success in fitness is about making it a lifestyle. As an entrepreneur, your success won't likely come from any one project. It will be a result of what you've done day in and day out for the past several months and years. A key factor in my success is consistency.

Now, all those factors were important to my success. But entrepreneurship required even more shifts in mindset. A big one was recognizing the value I had to offer.

I started out wondering, "Who's going to want to listen to me? What do I have to offer that's unique? Why would anyone buy my books or watch my videos if there are countless other people talking about the same subject?"

What shifted for me was recognizing that people aren't buying your information. They're buying your perspective. They're buying your story. They're buying your style.

It made sense. There are many guitar players I love. Eddie Van Halen, Nuno Bettencourt, Joe Satriani, Steve Vai, and more. And each player has his own unique style. There are no limits on the number of musicians I'd listen to. And people love hearing from many different authors, speakers, coaches, and mentors as well.

Even if a million other people are teaching what you have to teach, you can always have your own unique spin on it. Have you heard someone say something you've heard before, but for some reason, when they said it, it finally "clicked"? You never know if someone needs to hear a particular message coming from you.

Now, imagine you're a doctor on a plane. You hear a call on the intercom: "Is there a doctor on board?"

You go to a flight attendant, and she says, "We need your help. A passenger is dying."

At that moment, you use your skills to save this passenger's life. Now, it doesn't matter how many other doctors there are in the world. In that situation, you're the only doctor who matters. You become the most important person in the world to this individual.

I believe, as entrepreneurs, messengers, and world-changers, we have the ability to save people's lives. In some cases literally, and in other cases emotionally or financially. You may think many others can do what you do. And yet, for one person, in one situation, at one moment in time, you may be the only person who matters. Own this, and you'll believe in your value.

What is an unusual habit you have as an entrepreneur, and how does it help you persevere?

The most powerful habit I have is my three-magic-words technique. This technique breaks through procrastination, fear, and overwhelm.

I developed this technique based on the research of Stanford Behavior Scientist B. J. Fogg. He uses a concept called Tiny Habits, which is a type of micro-commitment. A micro-commitment is a very small task you commit to. In fitness, it may be just doing one push-up or putting on your workout shoes.

The technique works like this: You ask yourself, "Can I just...?" and then insert a micro-commitment.

Let's say I have an article I want to write, but I'm tempted to surf Facebook instead. I'd ask myself, "Can I just write the headline?"

It's a tiny action that will only take me about 20 seconds. Since it's so easy, I'll say, "Yes." If, for some reason, even that's too hard, I'll ask, "Can I just open my word processor and type nonsense for 10 seconds?"

Now, on the surface, that may seem pointless. Yet the magic happens because of the following principle: momentum generates motivation.

Have you ever resisted doing something, like exercising, only to find once you get started, you *want* to keep going? If you can "hack" the getting-started process by making it super easy, you'll be much more likely to continue the task almost effortlessly.

Since I often put off cleaning my apartment, I'll ask myself, "Can I just clean my desk?" Since it only takes a minute, I'll say, "Yes." Then once I feel the sense of completion, I'll ask, "Can I just clean my bathroom?" I'll often keep saying, "Yes," until next thing I know, I've effortlessly cleaned my whole apartment without feeling forced.

The key to a good micro-commitment is to make it easy. That means you're actually lowering your standards temporarily. For instance, "Can I just write one crappy paragraph?" Because you give yourself permission to do crappy work, it's easy to say, "Yes." Then you can keep asking, "Can I just do a little more?"

To make this work, you genuinely need to give yourself permission to quit after following through on the original micro-commitment. And you also want to reward yourself for any action you take.

Let's say you ask, "Can I just write one sentence?" If that's all you do, you still congratulate yourself. You could tell yourself out loud, "Nice work!" You could do a fist pump. Whatever you need to give yourself a hit of dopamine. You're training your brain to feel good for taking any action—no matter how small.

Your life may not change after just following through on one micro-commitment. But over time, you'll build belief in yourself. You'll shift your identity. You'll begin to see yourself as someone who follows through on your commitments. And when you follow through on the little things, you'll gain confidence and excitement to follow through on even bigger things.

I use this in virtually every area of life. It has been a game changer. And it's the secret to persevering year after year because it's guaranteed to work. Remember, if the answer isn't "Yes" to the "Can I just...?" question, you rework the question until you find something you can and will do.

How have you used a book for your business?

I struggled for years as an aspiring entrepreneur with blogging, affiliate marketing, YouTubing, and more. None of them generated much income when I started. It was only after my third book, *50 Fitness Tips You Wish You Knew,* went on to become a #1 best-seller that everything changed.

Since then, books have generated a nice passive income stream. On average, a few thousand dollars per month. More importantly, books function as a lead-generation tool. They help me build my list. That can be by giving books away for free in exchange for an email. It can also come from selling books, and then having people go from the book to a special offer I make inside the book for a freebie.

Books are also useful for positioning you as an expert. When I reach out to podcasts and publications to write in, I can leverage the fact I'm a #1 best-selling author.

I like to use books to warm up potential clients. You can use a book to overcome limiting beliefs in your prospects. You can use books to teach people what you want them to know before they become clients of yours.

If you keep finding yourself saying the same thing over and over again to people, you can save a lot of time by putting those concepts into a book. Then you direct people to your book instead of constantly repeating yourself. So when people say, "I don't have a lot of time to write a book," often that's exactly why they should write a book. To free up their time and gain leverage.

Another psychological benefit I've found from having a book is I now feel okay turning away people I don't want to work with. It was hard for me because I wanted to help everyone. Even those who couldn't afford me or would be a pain to work with. Now I'm able to direct people to my books, and I know they'll still get help even if they're not a good fit to become a client.

How do you make money from your books? How do you ensure this will continue to happen?

Books generate money from sales on Amazon. And most of those sales come from running Amazon ads. In addition to that, many sales come from my email list. My email list is the main focus of my business. Books build my list, and my list drives book sales.

Another great source of income is with audiobooks. I've generated thousands of dollars in passive royalties from audiobook sales. Many of these sales come from sites that I've never sent traffic to. So this is 100 percent passive as far as I'm concerned. The books are just out there making money from people discovering them organically.

So while some people say, "You can't make money from book sales," I'd argue that you can at least make a nice supplemental income. And, of course, there are a few authors whose primary source of income comes from books if they are consistently publishing.

Still, I get the sentiment that books aren't a big money maker. That's why most money comes from offering other products like courses and coaching. Books set you up to get more leads on autopilot. And, in some cases, you even get paid for those leads since people are investing money in your book.

One of the biggest sources of books sales for me comes from influencers. I noticed almost all the books I buy come from recommendations from people I trust. So the key is to start thinking about who's already built an audience of your ideal readers. Then figure out ways for them to promote your book to their audience. This will help you reach far more people with less effort when you get others promoting your book for you.

What bad advice do you often hear on the subject of authorship or writing a book for your business?

The "a book is just a business card" mentality isn't something I believe in. Yes, a book *is* a business card. And one of the best ones. But if you treat it as nothing more than a business card, you can work very hard on creating a bulky business card that gets ignored. All because you're not treating it as something far greater for you and your business than a credibility booster.

For instance, I received a book from a man at a seminar. I won't say the title, but it's not much better than a generic "How to be successful" type of book. Now, this book may serve the author well purely from the standpoint of his being able to say he's an author for credibility purposes. But I wouldn't ever read the book. I doubt others would either unless they know him personally. There's nothing captivating about the topic. There's no unique hook. And since that book won't get read, it did nothing for me to learn more about him, his business, and what he may offer.

I've heard people say you shouldn't expect your book to get read. Sadly, it's true that most people probably won't read your book.

Still, I personally love it when I get emails from readers saying how one of my books changed their lives. How they've recommended my book to their friends. How they want to work with me now because of my book. I pour my heart and soul into writing some of my books because I know how books have changed my life. I want every book I publish to get read and make an impact even if someone doesn't buy anything else from me.

Therefore, I believe in writing books that not only position you as an expert, but they also get read, reviewed, and recommended to others. And that's the approach I take when working with authors. Helping them create a book that people will want to read. A book that will make an impact.

In order to do this, it means taking the time to figure out how you're going to position your book in the marketplace so it stands out. It means understanding how to create compelling copy (the words that sell) so prospects are hungry to buy the book and read it. And it means collaborating with other influencers who will recommend people buy and read your book.

If you lost everything—your book, your list, your products, your platform, your fame—and nobody knew who you were, what would you do in the next 30 days to get back on track, and what role would a book or publication take in the process?

Fortunately, you aren't losing "everything" if you still have one of your greatest assets: your knowledge. So assuming I haven't also lost my knowledge, I'd focus on what I still have: my ability to help others.

I'd put the word out there that I want to help three people develop their best-selling book ideas. And I'd offer to train three people as a group on a Zoom call for a few hours for free in exchange for their feedback and testimonials.

This training would be enough to get them moving forward but couldn't cover every single thing I know about book creation and marketing. It would help them with the first piece of the process. And I'd ensure they'd have some sort of breakthrough on this training. I'd take this training and turn it into a book and mini-course to offer as a lead magnet.

Then I'd use the testimonials I get from those initial students as social proof to start reaching out to influencers. I'd really get to know an influencer, what they value, and how I can help them. Then I'd record a short one-to-two-minute video introducing myself. This will make me stand out from the crowd and show them I'm a real person.

From there, I'd hop on a call to see how I can best serve them and their audiences. Ideally, that would be doing a webinar. But it may also simply be writing a guest blog post for them, doing a free Facebook live training, coming on their podcasts, or offering to feature them in an upcoming product I'd create.

Technically, I could start with reaching out to influencers from the get-go. However, as an influencer myself, when people reach out to me, I want to know two things. The first is that they know what they're talking about. The second is that they can transfer that knowledge to others. I don't want my audience's time wasted with someone who can't skillfully teach.

So it's worth my taking an afternoon to train some other people and get their testimonials. That way an influencer can see I have the ability to train others.

My main focus would be on negotiating a free webinar to do for their audience with an affiliate partnership. The webinar would begin to grow my list, and the offer would let me sell a course I've yet to create.

To recap:

- I'd help a few people in exchange for their feedback.
- I'd turn this one training into a free book/course.
- I'd use this free book/course to generate leads.
- I'd invite those who opt in to my list to a webinar.

- I'd also reach out to potential affiliates to drive traffic to the webinar and/or lead magnet.
- And, from the webinar, I'd sell them a course I've yet to create.

The key thing to take away is the principles. Focusing on, "What can I give?" (Not just "What can I get?") Asking, "How can I stand out?" to get people's attention. And being able to sell the vision first, then creating the product later.

You can reach Derek at bestsellersecrets.com.

15

KEEP THE END RESULT IN MIND BY ASHLEY EMMA

What is your business?

Fearless Publishing House.

What is an unusual habit you have as an entrepreneur, and how does it help you persevere?

I say no to most things that people ask me to do. Sorry, I know that's probably not what you want to hear, but writing and publishing is a priority for me right now. It won't always be like that once I reach my monetary goal, but for right now, it is.

People always ask me how I have time for writing with three kids ages one, two, and four, but I make it my priority. It's my job. You don't hear people asking others how they have time for their day job, right? You make time for it because it's on your calendar, and it's mandatory.

When people want me to go somewhere or do something during my kids' nap time or at night, I often tell them I'll be working, because those are my work hours. With three kids, I have very limited time to work, so I have to make the most of it.

I know this is temporary. I often give up fun things so I can work because I know that the book I'm working on will allow me to increase my royalties and build a better future for my kids.

I keep the end result in mind: financial freedom, which equals more time for family and friends.

First and foremost, I'm a stay-at-home mom, which I wouldn't have any other way, and being an author allows me to do it. I do my house-work, and I spend quality time with my kids when they are awake, and I don't even bother touching my laptop during that time because I know I'll get interrupted anyway. When the kids have a fun activity to keep them busy, like Play-Doh or puzzles, then maybe I'll sneak some work in, but I mostly work when they nap and after they go to bed, often until midnight every night.

Hey, the life of an entrepreneur is not always as glamorous as it seems, especially in the early years, when you're solely responsible for keeping little humans alive, happy, and healthy.

Another thing I used to do was leave the house to work several nights a week just to have uninterrupted work time. Our house is tiny, and I didn't have an office.

But then I realized I could turn the closet downstairs into an office, so I cleared it out, donated several boxes of stuff, and made enough room for a desk and chair. I decorated the "office" beautifully, so it's where I love to spend time, and even put a rug and space heater in there to warm it up since we have such freezing cold winters here.

Whenever I need to do deep work, I ask my husband to watch the kids, and I go downstairs and shut the door, putting white noise on so

I don't hear anything. I know if I hear one of my kids crying, I'll run right up the stairs, so I need that white noise on. I remind myself that my husband is taking good care of them, and I don't have to worry.

I just shut out the rest of the world, focus, and get stuff done.

I wish I would have made this office a long time ago. If you don't have an office and think you don't have room for one, you might be surprised. If you can get rid of some stuff and clear out a closet, creating a small office where you can do deep work might be game-changing for you.

How have you used a book for your business?

I used my book, *Fearless Author*, to launch my self-publishing company, Fearless Publishing House. Within the first month of publishing *Fearless Author*, I generated over $17,000 worth of client work and booked myself out for several months. I did this by putting a link to my online calendar in the book, offering free consultations.

It has continued to grow so much faster than I ever imagined thanks to that book. Ever since I started the company over two years ago, I've had plenty of clients to work with, sometimes even more than I can handle. I've had to raise my prices more times than I can even recall.

Yes, I've had very stressful months where I didn't know how I'd ever have the time to complete all the projects I'd taken on. Yes, I've given up time with my husband and kids just to work crazy hours. My busiest work month ever was the month my third child was born.

But it's been worth it. So worth it.

I love helping aspiring authors achieve their dreams, market their books, and get their messages out to the world. It's truly such rewarding work.

How do you make money from your books? How do you ensure this will continue to happen?

First off, I make most of my income from publishing books for my clients in my company, Fearless Publishing House. My clients usually find me through referrals and word of mouth, but many of them find me through my books, especially *Fearless Author* or *Legit Work-At-Home Jobs*.

As far as book sales, about 90 percent of my royalties come from my Amish series, *The Covert Police Detectives Unit Series.* Now that I just released the third book in the series, sales for all my books have gone up significantly. Readers love series! The more books in a series, especially fiction, the better. When readers see a new book that is the third or fourth or fifth book in a series, they will often go back and buy all the other books.

I can now tell just by looking at past months' royalties how much I will earn on average per book per month, so that tells me how many books I need to publish in that series in order to reach my goal. I am about three books away from my goal, all of which are written but need editing. And one of those I am releasing in about a month.

Then I'll continue to publish more and more books, creating more and more Amish series. I plan on releasing an Amish fairytale series soon to branch out a bit from the Amish crime series. I love retold fairytales, so I'm super excited! They are still, of course, in the Amish genre. I've noticed it's important for me personally to continue publishing under the same genre because I sell more books that way.

Amazon ads and Facebook ads are what have tremendously increased my royalties over the past six months or so, but my recent success is mostly due to Amazon ads. You can learn to do them yourself through online courses or you could hire a professional, which is what I do, so

I can focus more on my writing. Marketing, marketing, marketing is key.

My husband is so supportive of my author career. He's my biggest fan and encourager. Whenever I have a big breakthrough with my books, I always tell him first.

About a year ago, he realized how much potential there was for success with my author business. I was feeling overwhelmed with getting my next book published, doing work for clients, and taking care of the kids. I wouldn't have it any other way, but it does get tough sometimes.

"What can I do to help?" he asked.

"Well, I bought a course on Facebook ads a few months ago and tried to do it, but I just can't wrap my head around it," I explained. "It's too technical for me. I don't have time to do it anyway."

"I'll do it for you!" he offered. "I'll do the course and set up your ads. Or, I'll try, at least." He was a bit unsure if he could do it since Facebook Ads is a huge learning curve.

He did the entire course in about a week, set up my Facebook ads for my books, and a year later, they are still running strong with only a few tweaks needed, costing only pennies per click. Those ads doubled my royalties!

If you're feeling overwhelmed, maybe someone in your family can help you. Don't be afraid to ask for help. You might be surprised by what your kids can help you with, and it is such a great learning opportunity for them. They might be able to use social media to help you with your business by posting in Facebook groups when your book is on sale. Maybe they can write your emails for you. Or maybe you can show them how a book is produced—like how to get it formatted and how the cover is made. It can show them how to run an author business, and who knows? Maybe when they grow up they'll want to be an author just like you.

I plan on homeschooling my kids, and when they're older, I definitely plan on involving them in my online businesses. What an awesome, unique, hands-on learning experience!

I've also used Facebook Ads and BookFunnel to grow my email list in a huge way. I just used the ads my husband made and redirected them to the landing page on my website where people can join my email list in exchange for free Amish books. I now have over 12,000 subscribers, which is a massive reason why I can sell so many books, especially when I release a new one and tell my list about it.

You've probably heard before that as an author, it's important to have an email list, and it's true. If you're serious about being a full-time author, you need to build an email list.

No excuses. Do it. You'll thank yourself a few years from now.

What bad advice do you often hear on the subject of authorship or writing a book for your business?

I often hear that "real" authors get published by traditional publishers, and the ones who aren't good enough just self-publish. Whenever I go to writers' conferences, self-publishing gets a bad rap. They say self-published books have typos, and you can't make money with self-publishing.

Man, that annoys me. It really irritates me.

Then I tell them about my books, and they are shocked.

"You're killing it," one traditionally published author told me at the last conference I went to. "I'm pretty sure you've sold more books than I have."

When I tell them I have 12,000 email subscribers, they're shocked. Some traditionally published authors don't even have an email list.

I know. Crazy.

The fact is, tons of traditionally published books don't sell nearly as well as self-published books. But I'm not saying all traditionally published books are like that, because I know many wildly successful traditionally published authors. It goes both ways.

Okay, I've seen plenty of self-published books that really do have awful covers and terrible (or nonexistent) editing. There are those.

But they do not represent all self-published books.

The self-published authors I know take great pride in the production of their books, and those are the authors who are changing the entire publishing industry.

It used to be that agents wouldn't even consider self-published authors, but now they do. The industry is changing. And if you have an email list and a following, that sure helps.

I think if you want to self-publish *and* traditionally publish, that's so awesome. That's what I do, and I love it. Whatever you do, take pride in your work and do the absolute best you can.

If you lost everything—your book, your list, your products, your platform, your fame—and nobody knew who you were, what would you do in the next 30 days to get back on track, and what role would a book or publication take in the process?

First of all, let me be honest. That is my worst nightmare. I'd panic. I'd completely freak out. I'd probably have a mental breakdown, cry for a few hours (or a few days, let's be real), then eventually, I'd get it together enough to do something about it.

I had a small taste of this when I accidentally deleted (don't even ask me how) half of my first Amish novel. I remember I was riding in the car with my husband, and I opened my laptop in the car to write and realized my entire book was gone. I had just finished writing the first draft only a few days before.

I had a full-blown panic attack. That was a miserable day to say the least.

I found the first half on a thumb drive, but it was an older version, so I had to edit it back to the way it was before. Then I locked myself in our dingy apartment and rewrote the second half of the book in about a week. (This was before I had kids. I probably wouldn't be able to do that now.)

It was the worst feeling in the world to open that laptop and realize everything I'd worked on for the past several months, what I'd poured myself into, was gone. It was the absolute worst.

But I rewrote it and published in a few short months, and that book is still my most popular book. It's the book that launched my career as an Amish fiction author, *Undercover Amish.*

Would I do it again? Of course. I would do anything to get back to where I am today.

I think if I lost absolutely everything related to my author career, after panicking, I would rewrite all my books, or as many as I could in 30 days. I'd probably have to leave town and turn off my phone so I could work without any interruptions.

I'd use Facebook Ads and BookFunnel to rebuild my list quickly, and I'd run contests and giveaways to get more subscribers.

I'd slowly republish each book one by one, skipping all the stupid mistakes I made the first time around, like writing in too many genres and having way too many beta readers who weren't professionals.

Now that I know you really can make money with this, I'd borrow money from someone to cover the publishing costs if I was broke. I'd publish my Amish series first, then *Fearless Author* and *Legit Work-at-Home Jobs* to continue getting leads for my publishing company.

It would be hard, especially to try to do it quickly. I'd say no to absolutely everything else, like social gatherings, going out to eat, and seeing friends (only temporarily), to make more time for rebuilding my empire. Basically, I'd hide in a cave somewhere until I was done.

My author career is so incredibly important to me. Being a full-time author has been my dream since I was little.

I'd do whatever it took to get it back to the way it was, even if I had to make huge sacrifices until I got there.

I'd just remember this quote: "If you will live like no one else, later you can live like no one else."

— Dave Ramsey

The hardest part would be just getting started, but I think if I just powered through and got it done quickly, I know I'd be so happy I did it later on.

Even now, I often skip cookouts or other fun things so that my husband can take the kids to them, and I get an entire day of work done with no interruptions. I might be a nerd, but I love days where I can work on my books all day long.

So yes, it would be hard. Even now it's hard, but I know in a few years I'll look back and be so glad I did this for myself and my family.

You can reach Ashley at ashleyemmaauthor.com.

16

THE RIGHT ATTITUDE AND MENTAL FORTITUDE BY JEFF HILDERMAN

What is your business?

All-Star Academy.

What have been the key factors to your success and why?

I believe success is a game we play with ourselves, and the rules are always changing. It's human nature to continuously redefine what it looks like, why we want it, and how we'll get it as our priorities change over time. But as I reflect on my own personal success, I've also come to realize there are also a number of constants to this game—things that I've consistently done (and not done), to which I credit much of my success.

There are certain attributes which are a given to be successful in life: purpose, work ethic, perseverance, optimism, and so on. The mental game is where it all begins and, too often, where it ends. Multiply anything by zero and what do you have? Zero. Likewise, without the right attitude and mental fortitude to accomplish your goals, success will remain just out of reach.

But, of course, you know this. Whether you're a seasoned entrepreneur or aspiring to become one, I'm going to assume you already have the right mindset. If you didn't, you probably wouldn't be reading this book. So let's jump ahead to the physical part of the equation where the rubber meets the road.

I've narrowed down my success to three tangible actions that anyone can take. Regardless of who you are, what you do, or the dreams you have, take these three things to heart, and success will follow you wherever you go.

#1: Write Down Your Goals . . . Seriously

While I don't consider myself a new-age kind of guy, I do believe in the Law of Attraction: the theory that we attract whatever we focus on. It seems like more than a coincidence that negative people always have the worst luck. Or that when you're in the market for something new, like a vehicle, an outfit, or a pet, you all of a sudden see it everywhere. We attract what we're focused on.

Jim Carrey popularized this theory by sharing his own personal story, where he wrote himself a check for $10 million after dreaming of becoming a mainstream actor. He post-dated the check for 10 years, and, remarkably, 10 years later, he made $10 million for his role in *Dumb and Dumber*.

To be clear, I'm not suggesting you write yourself a check for millions of dollars and then wait it out. What I'm really saying is to write down your goals, no matter how big and ridiculous they may feel, and then work at it every single day. Trust yourself and the process, and your unwavering determination will be rewarded in unexpected ways.

When I set out to write my best-selling book, *Clone Yourself,* the very first thing I did was pull out a calendar and determine my launch date. At the time, all I had was an idea and a deadline, but that's all I needed to get started. There was no way for me to know exactly how long it would take for me to publish my first book, but it didn't matter. I wrote down my goal and worked at it every day because it was a priority.

Whether you believe in the Law of Attraction or not, most would agree that goals without deadlines are just dreams. If it matters, write it down and declare it to yourself (bonus points for saying it out loud). And while you're at it, make sure your goals are specific, measurable, attainable, relevant, and time-bound, because that's the S.M.A.R.T. thing to do.

#2: Build a Routine Around Your Goal

Good or bad, we all have routines. But the question to ask yourself is if your present routine is aligned with your future success. Most people fall short of their goals because they try to fit them into their existing (and comfortable) routine instead of restructuring their day around their new priorities.

A recent study published in the *European Journal of Social Psychology* showed that on average, it takes 66 days to form positive habits, and within that time, we're most susceptible to failure. (FOOTNOTE: Lally, P., van Jaarsveld, C. H. M., Potts, H. W. W. and Wardle, J. (2010), How are habits formed: Modeling habit formation in the real world. Eur. J. Soc. Psychol., 40: 998-1009. doi:10.1002/ejsp.674)

This is why structure and success go hand in hand. Your new routine must be rigid enough to promote consistency and promote positive habits, but also flexible enough to accommodate the rest of your life; otherwise, you're just setting yourself up for failure.

I wouldn't be where I am today without my morning routine. My power hour, the time when I'm at peak focus, energy, and performance, is within the first two hours of my day. So how do I use this to my advantage? By waking up one to two hours earlier than everybody else and using my most productive time to work on my personal goals when I know I won't be interrupted. This is exactly how I published my book and built my side-business: one hour at a time.

Don't worry, if you're not a morning person, you can still build a routine around your goals. The trick is to identify when your power hour is and align it with your personal goals. Carve it out, make it sacred, and don't let yourself off the hook. After approximately 66 days, you'll find your new groove and have time every day set aside for deep, focused work.

#3: Shift Gears from Me to We

Like many entrepreneurs, I bought into the notion that to be successful you had to work really hard, wear all these hats, and basically do everything yourself. But everything changed in 2008 when I burned out at work, became a first-time father, and lost my sister unexpectedly when she was only 25. After developing an anxiety disorder and struggling to be the person I needed to be at work and at home, I knew I had to make some big changes in my life.

I needed to improve my health; that was a given. But I also wanted to go to work feeling inspired and put my energy into the things I loved. I didn't want my job to be stressful anymore; I wanted it to be fun and exciting. And most importantly, I wanted to spend more time with my family and friends and even take up a few hobbies. In other words, I wanted my freedom back.

So over the next year or two, I tried all sorts of things to improve my situation. I read dozens of personal development books, I attended workshops and joined professional groups but saw little progress. The frustration continued to grow until I had an epiphany.

One day, I was rummaging through my desk when I came across notes from a seminar I attended. As I flipped through the ideas I had written down, I couldn't help but feel discouraged that I never had the time to implement them, and then it hit me. Why didn't I have time? What was standing in my way? And that's when I realized that I was the problem; I had unknowingly become the bottleneck of the business. And the more I thought about it, the more it made perfect sense.

The reason I didn't have the time and energy to focus on the big picture was because I was fixated on the small picture. This was the missing piece of the puzzle. All the experts talk about working on your business instead of in it, but nobody was talking about how to make this transition—particularly in the real world. Consequently, I found my second wind and set out to remove myself from the day-to-day operations so I could finally achieve the goals I had set for myself back in 2009.

And 18 months later, I got there. I reclaimed my freedom and was back to doing what I love: planning for the future. I no longer felt the need to be in control of everything because I had a team who understood my vision and could bring it to life. Best of all, I was able to significantly reduce my work hours and spend more time with my wife and our three cool kids.

What I learned from all of this is that you can't do epic things with an average team, and you certainly can't do it all yourself. There are people out there who understand your vision, share your passion, and can even run your business for you. There are mentors out there who've walked in your shoes and can help you go further and faster than doing it on your own. But this doesn't happen by accident. It begins with you and the decision to mentally shift gears from me to we—that's when the magic happens.

What is an unusual habit you have as an entrepreneur, and how does it help you persevere?

Something unusual about me is that I do my best work in busy environments. This goes back to my university days when I found it impossible to study anywhere quiet. I would feel a wave of drowsiness come over me within minutes of setting foot in a quiet library or classroom. My dorm wasn't a possibility either, given the ever-present distractions.

But then I discovered coffee shops. There was something soothing about hearing people work and chat in the background. It was loud enough to keep me alert, but never bothersome. In fact, I found that the louder my environment, the easier it was for me to focus. Starbucks became my second home until I graduated. I was there so often that I became friends with everyone who worked there; they even gave me a signed picture to remember them by.

Since then, I've carried on with this tradition. While I now do the majority of my work in my studio, I still need to escape to a busy place when I really need to focus on something. Not surprisingly, I wrote *Clone Yourself* in another Starbucks, which I suppose explains my addiction to coffee.

How have you used a book for your business?

Publishing a book changed my life in ways I couldn't have imagined. In school, we're taught about the Big Bang Theory, which explains how the entire universe came from a singularity. This is exactly how I see my book, the genesis for everything that came after: All-Star Academy, coaching programs, workshops, and speaking opportunities—all of it.

Shortly after hitting best-seller status, a lot of people reached out to me wanting to know more about my story and my business. Honestly, I didn't even know how to respond because there *was* no business, not yet anyway.

It sounds silly, but it never occurred to me that others saw me as an expert. Why would they? I was just a regular guy who shared his experience and few things he learned along the way. But the more I thought about it, the more I realized an expert wasn't somebody who had everything figured out. Instead, an expert simply had more expertise than somebody else—more knowledge, more experience, and certainly more failures.

In other words, an expert is just a regular person who's a few steps ahead of somebody else. This is why a book can easily turn into a business or propel an existing one forward. A published book creates instant credibility as an expert in your field. And if people resonate with your message and your ideas, and they believe you can help them, you can!

There are many ways you can use a book in your business. For me, *Clone Yourself* serves as the foundation for everything I do. The framework and strategies found inside are the same I use for my coaching program, webinars, and workshops. The core message is the same whether I'm talking to one person or a hundred.

I also use my book as a business card, both figuratively and literally. I've handed it out at seminars, speaking events, and other professional functions. Again, it's a great credibility marker, and it also gets your book into the hands of people who wouldn't necessarily know who you are. Use your imagination on this one: potential clients and collaborators, editors, reporters, podcasters, video producers, and the gatekeepers to industry leaders. A personalized copy of your book is one of the easiest ways to get your foot in the door for publicity and future business.

How do you make money from your books? How do you ensure this will continue to happen?

I'm asked all the time if you can make money writing books, particularly in the self-publishing world. Of course you can! However, the amount you will make is harder to predict given the number of variables at play, such as: the quality of your book, your reviews, niche, competition, demand, and the time of year. Well-known authors can make thousands of dollars a day because they have the platform and following to drive those sales. However, if you're just starting out, you should expect a fraction of this.

Now, before you get discouraged, consider the long game. Where do you see yourself and your business five to 10 years from now? If you envision yourself on stage giving a TED talk or behind the microphone of your very own podcast, you can bet the evergreen exposure will continue to funnel people to your book for years to come. Likewise, if you see additional books in your future, it's fair to assume they will promote one another as your fan base grows over time.

But here's the deal: The real money isn't in the book; it's in the business behind the book. Think about how many books you'd have to promote and sell to make $5,000 versus giving an hour-long keynote for the same amount of money. For me, I have a steady passive income from my ebook, paperback, and audiobook, but it's a drop in the bucket compared to my high-ticket private coaching program. And when All-Star Academy's flagship course is released, I expect my book sales to become negligible altogether.

So why bother publishing a book at all, you might ask? Because your purpose should revolve around impact, not money. Understand that 99.99 percent of the population isn't going to buy your high-ticket item or subscribe to your services—especially if they don't know, like, and trust you. They will, however, part ways with a few bucks if they're attracted to your book. It's the perfect low-cost, high-value product you can offer to make a difference in somebody's life. And if you exceed their expectations, you'll have another opportunity to nurture your relationship and make another much larger sale down the road.

What bad advice do you often hear on the subject of authorship or writing a book for your business?

Self-publishing coaches will often tell you that done is better than perfect, but I would take this advice with a grain of salt. It's true that if you're striving for perfection, your book will never see the light of day. But there's a fine line between accepting your work for what it is versus what it could be. Many self-publishing programs promote a 90-day (or less) turnaround time. Is it possible to publish a book in that time? Sure is, but I wouldn't recommend it.

I know it's tempting to crank out your book as quickly as possible and claim the coveted best-selling badge of honor. But remember, your book reflects the quality of your work across the board. If it's fluffy, confusing, strung together, or feels unprofessional, your readers will assume the rest of your work is, too.

Like I said, take the advice with a grain of salt. Done is better than perfect, but great is also better than good. Put your heart into your book, and make it the best it can be. Set a reasonable goal (anywhere from six months to a year), do your research, find your voice, and go the extra mile to exceed their expectations. Years from now, your release date won't matter, but the quality of your product and its lasting impact will.

If you lost everything—your book, your list, your products, your platform, your fame—and nobody knew who you were, what would you do in the next 30 days to get back on track, and what role would a book or publication take in the process?

I'm at ground zero of my business apocalypse, and I've lost it all: my book, my products, my customers, and my platform. But after a brief, ugly cry, I realize that everything is still in my head, and I can turn it all around in 30 days. I pick myself up, brew a pot of coffee, and put my game face on. It's go time.

Day 1: The Blueprint

Today's agenda is strategic planning on steroids. There's a lot to figure out and no time to waste, but fortunately, I have something else that survived the apocalypse—my WHY. I already know that I'm driven to help entrepreneurs build businesses they love. I also know that my passion and my experience intersect at leadership coaching. So I decide to create a high-ticket coaching program, which is my best shot at maximizing my profit and my impact in just 30 days.

Normally, I'd spend a lot of time researching and validating my ideas, but I'm on a deadline, so an hour of online detective work is all I can afford. I find a few people who are already doing what I want to do. I study their copy, their lead magnets, their funnels, and their target audience. Then I reverse engineer this process and figure out how to put a spin on it to differentiate myself from everybody else.

After a full day of planning, I have a rough outline of my business mapped out on paper. It's not perfect, but I've figured out:

- My Ideal Customer: their wants, needs, opportunities, challenges, and pain points.
- My Offer: my group coaching program, freebies, bonuses, and workflow.
- My Message: the core message I will use to market my coaching program.
- My Story Bank: my signature story and other relatable stories and examples.
- My Brand: my company name, tag line, value proposition, personal bio, and a domain for my website.
- My Platform: where and how I'll capture leads.

Day 2: D-Day (Decision Day)

Yesterday was a major brain dump, and today, I need to firm up the details. After a little tweaking, I've finalized my plan.

My value proposition is that I'm a leadership coach who helps visionary entrepreneurs build their dreams and automate their businesses. I will offer a 12-week group-coaching program which includes a private Facebook group, weekly "business hours" where students can ask me anything, unlimited email support, and free access to all future content (which I eventually plan to turn into an online course). As a bonus, I also have a referral program offering a generous commission to past students who sign up new ones.

My private coaching program will be priced at $3,600, but since I have no social proof or testimonials, I need to do something special to enroll 12 students. I decide to market this as a beta-group and offer a special price of $1,800. A 50 percent discount is extremely attractive, and even then I'll still have $21,600 in the bank before the end of the month.

I plan to use Facebook ads and live videos as my primary source for leads. Furthermore, I'll join other groups where I believe my target audience is and answer questions to get on their radar.

Before the day is done, I also finalize my company's name, register the domain, create my legal business entity, and set up my online banking. Good day.

Days 3–5: Building the Foundation

The next three days are intense but extremely rewarding. Here's what I accomplish:

- I hire a freelancer on Fiverr to produce a company logo for me within 24 hours.
- I ask my wife to take a few professional headshots so I can edit them in Photoshop.
- I set up an account with Canva and create banners for my social media accounts.
- I set up my Instagram, LinkedIn, and Twitter accounts to secure my username.
- I set up an account with Kartra and build a basic sales funnel and website (Home, About, Coaching Services, and Contact Information).
- I set up a G Suite account and link it to Kartra's mail service.

Days 6 and 7: My Coaching Program

Today, I create my coaching program from the ground up. The first thing I do is map everything out so I don't forget anything.

I plan to have two different lead magnets that I'll use to split-test my Facebook ads: a quiz and a PDF checklist. I know video is the ultimate engagement tool, so I decide to repurpose a part of my first live video for my ad. This way I can capture their attention and deliver amazing value, and then promote my free offer below it.

After the person provides a valid email address, they'll be redirected to a thank you page featuring a quick video about my coaching program. Below it, you'll see a call to action to book a free 30-minute clarity call with me. Once I set up Calendly, the person will be able to book an appointment with me with a single click. I'll also create a follow-up email sequence inside my autoresponder to re-engage anyone who downloaded my lead magnet but didn't book an appointment.

Now I need to look at the actual workflow of my coaching program. I'll need a coach-client contract, but I can buy a template online and modify it accordingly, so that's easy. As for the content itself, I plan on creating a new module each week based on the feedback of my students. However, I still need to outline a preliminary 12-week roadmap with a brief synopsis so my students know what to expect, so that's the next thing I do. I also come up with the content for my first module to get the ball rolling, along with a slide deck and a few downloadable resources.

Next, I think about the onboarding process and come up with a little welcome package that I'll upload inside each students' Google Drive account. I'll also need to make another email sequence to orientate my students and get them fired up. Afterward, I come up with a running list of everything I need to do, which also includes:

- Creating my marketing material.
- Outlining the format of our weekly meetings and to develop a Session Itinerary.
- Setting up a Zoom account with a recurring Google Calendar appointment.

- Creating a private Facebook group with a welcome video and community guidelines.

I manage to get everything knocked off with a little time to spare, so I decide to spend the rest of my day with my family and clear my head.

Day 8: Finding My Tribe

With my infrastructure in place and a million housekeeping tasks behind me, I can finally turn my attention to my target audience. My primary goal over the next two weeks is to get on people's radar by providing tons of valuable content. I know the key to pulling this off is to be consistent with my actions, so I make a daily checklist:

- Spend one hour in the morning answering questions in Facebook groups.
- Outline my talking points for my Facebook Live video and promote it in advance.
- Create two to three stories on Instagram and Facebook (mix it up between work and personal).
- Post once a day on both platforms to create engagement.

Now that I've allocated two to three hours each day for social media, I need to come up with the content. Because I'm using a portion of my first video for my ad campaign, it's the perfect opportunity to tell my signature story and touch on my coaching services. I really want to knock this one out of the park, so I reach out to my friends and family and humbly ask them to engage in my video. Facebook will pick up on their questions, comments, likes, and shares and, consequently, show my video to more people.

After working out what I'm going to say, I decide to postpone my first Facebook Live until tomorrow. It's been a long week, and frankly, I'm exhausted. I know I need to bring my A-game tomorrow, so I take the rest of the day off to rest and recover.

Day 9: Showtime

Today's the day! I feel re-energized and knock off my daily checklist with ease. I'm not going live until tonight, so I spend some extra time double-checking everything. Next, I set up my camera and microphone, adjust my lighting, and carefully prepare my backdrop. I review my notes one last time and blast my social media accounts to let everyone know I'm about to go live.

It's now the moment of truth. I go live, and after a few minutes, the butterflies go away, and I'm in the zone. I didn't get as much engagement as I had hoped for, but I remind myself this was the very first one, and it's going to take some time to get traction. The good news is that I have views and comments trickling in, so I take the time to field additional questions and stir up the engagement. I'm excited, nervous, and relieved all at the same time, and I have to force myself to go to sleep.

Day 10: Back to the Grindstone

I eagerly check Facebook as soon as I wake up, and to my delight, I discover the likes and comments have tripled overnight, and I even have a few shares. This is fantastic news, and my confidence goes through the roof.

Unfortunately, the celebration is short-lived because I have a ton of work to do today. After thanking my friends and family for helping me out last night, I crush my daily checklist. Next, I edit my Facebook Live video and create my campaign and retargeting ads. It takes longer than expected, but I still have enough time to collect my thoughts before my second live video. Once again, I go live, and this time, I don't even feel nervous.

After another engaging discussion, I sign off with a call to action: I ask my audience to comment on future topics they'd like me to talk about. This will allow me to validate my material and ensure that I'm speaking about things they actually care about. I've already made up my mind not to promote my coaching services for two weeks, with the exception of the brief mention in my first video. Right now, it's critical to give A LOT before I ask for anything in return.

Days 11–21: Full Steam Ahead

My new goal is consistency. Every day, I need to show up and engage my audience, whether that's within Facebook groups, live videos, or stories. I'm also more active on Instagram, where I've started a daily "Ask Me Anything" segment.

Everything begins to fall into place as my videos garner more likes, shares, and comments. I also continue to tweak my ad campaigns, which are now steadily bringing in a few clarity calls a day. Best of all, by the end of Week 3, I've managed to close my first two clients. I'm ecstatic!

During this time, I'm careful not to push myself too hard because if my health takes a dive, my business will, too. I make time for my family every day, which keeps me grounded throughout this crazy adventure.

Day 22: Shifting Gears

Today, I map out my goals and tasks for the rest of the month. It's time to shift gears and actively promote my coaching services, so I outline my next videos around my target audience's aspirations and pain points.

I plan to go deep with the first video of my new series and retell my signature story. I know I've picked up more viewers over the past weeks, so it's critical to re-establish an emotional connection with them. I will also touch on what to expect in the upcoming videos and tease about a new opportunity coming soon. In my call to action, I ask everyone to share my video and tag anyone who should see it.

In Video 2, I will pull back the curtain on my coaching program and paint a picture of where I can take my students. I'll also share relatable stories and examples to highlight my credibility markers and create buy-in. My call to action in every video moving forward will be to sign up for my free offer and book a clarity call with me. To create scarcity, I'll also let everyone know that I'm only accepting 12 people so I can dedicate my full attention to the group.

The remaining videos will echo the second, but I will also encourage a few viewers to jump on live with me to share their stories. I'll help them work through a problem in real time and reach out to them afterward to book a clarity call.

Days 23–27: The Final Countdown

I put my new plan into motion, and things are looking great. My consistency has paid off, and by midweek, I've closed another four clients—I'm halfway there! Between my campaign ads, follow-up email sequence, and live videos, I'm nearly booked solid for clarity calls.

On Day 27, I still have three spots to fill, and I'm feeling less confident than I did a few days ago. But I keep telling myself that people often wait until the last minute before making a decision. After my daily checklist, I spend most of the day following up with potential clients on social media, email, and Facebook Messenger.

That evening, I give a final push on my last live video and really drive the scarcity home. I manage to close my final three clients, and I'm relieved beyond measure. I did it! By Day 27, I have $21,600 in the bank and three months of work ahead of me. Before I go to bed, I give a final shout-out to everyone for their support.

Days 28 and 29: Onboarding My Students

By comparison, the next two days are a breeze. I take a modest break from social media for a couple of days with the plan of showing up daily afterward for my new following. After all, I need to start nurturing new relationships for future group-coaching programs.

Today and tomorrow are primarily admin days. I review everyone's coach-client agreements to ensure everything is in order, and I confirm everyone is paid up. After that, I set up everyone's work folder in Google Drive and send a welcome email to the group. Our first coaching session begins on Monday, and we're all ready to go!

Days 30: Looking Ahead

Today, I have a few loose ends to tie up but nothing serious. My Facebook ad campaign did remarkably well, and after a few more tweaks, I keep it running. I make small changes inside my funnel as well and replace my "Book a Clarity Call" button with "Apply Now," which takes the person to an application form I created using Google Forms.

Everything else can wait. I'll have more than enough time between my coaching sessions to work on my business. I'll come up with next month's social media plan and start batching my content. I'll also create a nurturing campaign to warm up applicants on my waiting list. I have a million ideas to scale my business, and the sky is the limit. Hell, I might even publish a book.

You can reach Jeff at jeffhilderman.com.

17

ALWAYS SEE THE POSITIVE BY ELIZABETH HEBERT

What is your business?

Writer, creativity coach, blogger.

What have been the key factors to your success and why?

Understanding the mind, as well as mindset, and how to move beyond our perceived barriers.

What is an unusual habit you have as an entrepreneur, and how does it help you persevere?

I look for connections and synchronicities. In my mind, I ask lots of questions. Also, I always see the positive. I don't believe in failure. Everything is just information. We use this information to make judgments based on a preconceived notion of what success or failure looks like.

What if we stopped making judgments and just explored what is happening and what is being created? Years ago, an instructor in a watercolor class I enrolled in helped me to create what she called a "happy accident."

You see, watercolor is not forgiving like oil or acrylic. Once the pigment is on the paper, it is there, and you must work with it. She taught me to work with the colors that were not in the "plan," and when you let go, then, sometimes the results are better than you expect. Writing is sometimes like that. You don't know where the story is going. Ask different questions, and you get different answers.

How have you used a book for your business?

I use my books in my coaching to show people that you can achieve any goal.

How do you make money from your books? How do you ensure this will continue to happen?

Promotions and giveaways. Amazon promotions. Author Central and Facebook.

What bad advice do you often hear on the subject of authorship or writing a book for your business?

The advice I usually hear is that it is EASY. It isn't always. But if I were going to advise someone, I would say don't do what I did. Don't jump in without doing research. The focus I had was on completing my book for my satisfaction, and then I set out to release it to the public. I do not recommend this approach. Don't do what I did.

I was so thrilled just to be published that I did not do any research on publishing companies. Giving up power to a company that cared little for me or my story left me confused and uninspired. Their idea of promotion was nothing more than a silly press release. An author needs to think about emerging from obscurity and developing an author platform before publication. Today's author must know it is not only an art form but a business endeavor as well.

If you lost everything—your book, your list, your products, your platform, your fame—and nobody knew who you were, what would you do in the next 30 days to get back on track, and what role would a book or publication take in the process?

One can possibly repeat any event. Knowing success is possible can recreate that success. Hindsight is the compass necessary to expedite a repeat achievement. I could start promoting right away and build a bigger platform. Perhaps, this time, I would collaborate with someone to construct respectful and more fantastic products to help people.

You can reach Elizabeth at yourdreamesteem.com.

18

FOCUS BY EMILY HIRSH

What is your business?

I was 19 years old, pregnant with my son, and in college. I worked as a nanny—I've always been an entrepreneur, so I do have that going for me—but I didn't know anything about the online world. I wasn't majoring in marketing or anything. I just found this freelance site and applied to be a virtual assistant. I got one client, and it spiraled from there. I got into some Facebook groups and pretty soon had a dozen clients. I was saying yes to everything. Yes, I can do that. I can do whatever you want me to do. I said yes, then taught myself on YouTube so I would be able to learn how to do it.

Before I knew it, I was super valuable. I knew every software out there and how to run it. I started doing marketing, Facebook ads, and I'd support launches in the back end and funnels and even build their ads. I started getting great results, great cost per leads. I loved it. At the time, I was eating up Amy Porterfield's podcast and learning everything I could learn about marketing. I realized Facebook ads were what I wanted to focus on. I began only offering that for clients, and then that also grew. Before long, I had 1,215 clients on my own doing Facebook ads, and I knew I had to grow a team. This was about a year and a half ago.

At the time, I had no idea how to grow a team. I never thought I'd have full-time employees, but now I have 25. I have spent the last year and a half putting systems and processes in place to teach my team what I did really well, which is run ads and marketing. Also communication with clients is so important that I feel I have to teach that to people as well.

It's grown really fast, and people always ask me, did you know what you were going to do? No, I didn't. I just kind of fell into this. I'm really good at marketing, and I'm also a really driven entrepreneur, so I just kind of ended up on this journey.

We do everything for Facebook and Instagram ads, specifically helping influencers. We do all actual implementation, but also the strategy behind it. We also specialize in webinars and product launches, growing people's influence and following. That's all. We have over 65 clients. That's everybody. I've actually spent the last year getting really clear about that and saying no to people; it helped us scale a lot.

About a year ago, I realized nobody can do client strategy calls. How am I going to get out of this so the company can grow? My coach said I had to document my process. What I did was repeatable, but I had to be able to teach it. That was really hard because it's not a checklist. It's in my head; it's intuition. I'm just naturally thinking about strategy that way.

This led to me documenting what we call the Hirsch Process—how we run our client ads. It's how I train my team. Even when hiring people who have a lot of marketing experience, we put them through our training, which is a huge workbook. It's an entire course, really.

That's how I've been able to scale up to 12 ads managers who can all represent me in the process, instead of me actually being there.

You can really repeat what you're doing if you teach somebody.

What have been the key factors to your success and why?

Focus. Focus is really hard, but when you can focus on one audience you're serving and do it really, really, really well, instead of adding all these things that you do *kind of* well, you can grow so much faster because you're able to perfect what you're doing. I have slowly gotten rid of other streams of income to be the best ads agency in the influencer space.

The journey to $1 million is figuring out what your focus should be. Once you know you've hit a million doing that thing, don't add other things until you have totally tapped out of that market. I'm not even close to the point where we are working with every big influencer out there possible. We've not tapped the market, and we probably won't until $10 million or higher, if you look at the biggest marketing agencies. So it's stopping yourself when that thought comes up and asking yourself, have I fully tapped out the potential, or are there areas I can focus in on? Could I make my delivery better, or could I focus on my marketing? It's always yes.

Improvement gets boring. Honestly. It does. There are times when I just want to do a new project and launch something new, but it will impact the business.

It is super powerful when you can get a team focused and aligned—all working toward the same thing.

Ideas don't make millionaires. Execution does. If you can't execute your ideas, they mean nothing.

What is an unusual habit you have as an entrepreneur, and how does it help you persevere?

I'm very good at actually planning my day and being really strict about it. Even when I was a kid, I used to plan my day hour by hour. I think most entrepreneurs don't have that. They hate schedules. They hate calendars. They won't plan their day, but when I plan to that level, I'm able to get so much done.

How have you used a book for your business?

I love to read. I usually read a novel at night and a business book during the day. Right now, I read a lot of leadership books because that's my core focus. Leadership and team culture is so important, and I have so much to learn. I use books all the time for just growing my knowledge, especially in business. I definitely don't have a lot of experience. I've done a good job, but I'm 24 and haven't run a million-dollar company before, so I have so much to learn from experts out there. I can't read fast enough. I always have a stack of books, and I use it to kind of pass on that knowledge and train my team as needed.

How do you make money from your books? How do you ensure this will continue to happen?

I have not written a book yet. It's something I definitely want to do. I think it's a great way to build a relationship with people. I look at some of our really successful clients, Mel Robbins and Rachel Hollis —their books are what really exploded their brands and their relationships with people. If you want to be that level of influencer, you need a book.

I definitely will write a book when I can focus on it, but I'm not allowed to right now.

We do have case studies and things we send to clients. I guess it's a mini book. It's a pamphlet of the Hirsch Process we have documented as a trifold. We used to send that to what we call our Dream 100 Campaign. I send that in a video card that actually plays a video in the mail. My process is documented in that way so that we could have it be a PDF download or something and have that value. And then, the onboarding, I also obviously have that for my team. When they come on, they've got a massive workbook. That's another form of giving my knowledge.

What bad advice do you often hear on the subject of authorship or writing a book for your business?

I don't think it has to be perfect. People stress about that, but I think the faster you can get it out, especially if you have an amazing story or an amazing message, the better. They say that with everything—your first course or your first book should kind of suck, right? If it's perfect, you waited way too long to get it out there. People will resonate with imperfection.

People wait too long—myself included. I could make time for writing 30 minutes a day and probably get a book done. I've heard authors say setting aside that kind of daily time is good because then they can go over, but at least they started every day. I'll do that. I'm going to probably write a better one later on, but at least I got something out.

If you lost everything—your book, your list, your products, your platform, your fame—and nobody knew who you were, what would you do in the next 30 days to get back on track, and what role would a book or publication take in the process?

That's where I was four years ago. I had no knowledge of the online world, no relationships, no connections, no business foundation or anything. I just started building relationships. It works. Organic traffic can work and Dream 100 and all that. Relationships are everything.

All the growth I've had has come from building relationships, being in mastermind groups with the right people and delivering service to them, and building a good reputation. If you had nothing and no money, that's something free that you can do. You don't have "anything," but you have your knowledge, and you can start to spread that or your story and connect with people. It can be done. One step at a time.

When I first started, I found Facebook groups and said to myself, "Wow, this is a whole new world." Communities exist out there. Maybe it's an event, maybe it's a Facebook group, maybe it's a mastermind. Find some communities where you can meet people in bulk and talk to people. You never know where those relationships will go. Be consistent; don't show up once a month. Nobody will pay attention to that, but if you show up every day, you absolutely will gain traction.

Rachel Hollis goes on Facebook Live every single day with her husband and does *The Rachel and Dave Show*. They have built something organically that I've never seen before with followers and connections by being consistent and building relationships with their audience.

Right now, we're launching. I finally have been able to focus on it. Is it called Ignite. It's a Facebook Ads course teaching people how to do what we're doing. My team is teaching all those videos.

I do the first part of the strategy, which is the Hirsh Process broken down, very detailed. Then my team does the tactical parts on how to run ads. Then we have a launch section as well for live launches—specifically ads. It's everything we do. It's intended for somebody if they want to do it themselves, or if you have an in-house team. The strategy piece is so huge—the foundation. Ads don't work unless that works on the back end.

You can reach Emily at emilyhirsh.com.

19

ABSOLUTE EMPOWERMENT BY VERA MIRNA

What is your business?

Energy healing. I use energy to help people reprogram their subconsciouses toward success.

What have been the key factors to your success and why?

Identifying limiting unconscious programming and removing these blocks to clear the path toward unstoppable action-taking. Once I learned how to do this for myself, I made it my mission to teach others to do the same by creating easy-to-use tools that can be taught to anyone in less than five minutes but work for an entire lifetime.

What is an unusual habit you have as an entrepreneur, and how does it help you persevere?

I believe that I can do anything that anyone else can do. Anybody's mindset, business strategies, and life philosophy can be reverse engineered, understood, applied, and simplified as appropriate. I also believe that anything I can do, someone else can do as well. My clients find my belief in their absolute empowerment to be unique and refreshing.

How have you used a book for your business?

I create journals to help people keep their mindsets on track and to stay in the energy of gratitude on a daily basis.

How do you make money from your books? How do you ensure this will continue to happen?

During sessions with clients, I am able to recommend other products and services, including my journals. I can also recommend it during the follow-up email sequence that goes out after the private session.

What bad advice do you often hear on the subject of authorship or writing a book for your business?

The worst advice I have heard is to "publish and pray," where a person uses self-publishing platforms to upload their books without doing any further marketing or launch strategies to help the books be found.

If you lost everything—your book, your list, your products, your platform, your fame—and nobody knew who you were, what would you do in the next 30 days to get back on track, and what role would a book or publication take in the process?

Even if it seems like you've lost everything, there are some things that cannot be lost. These are your mindset and your skill set. Even without a book, or product, or reputation, your personal genius is and will always be intact.

As an energy healer, I have one of the most valuable skills in the world. I am able to help people remove energy blocks and limiting beliefs so that they know they are capable of anything. My clients have been able to use the simple tools I have created to manifest their dream lives, free houses, empowering relationships, fulfilling careers, perfect health, unexpected windfalls, and so much more. I have a skill set that is constantly in high demand and benefits everyone.

The first step of starting over is identifying my tribe, my base of clients that resonate with my message. With a time limit of 30 days, I need to find a way to speak with thousands of potential clients all at once to get my message out into the world as fast as possible. The best way I know how to do this is to identify podcasts and telesummits that have thousands of listeners interested in energy work and self-improvement. One of the major benefits from going in this direction instead of seeking in-person speaking opportunities is that there is no travel required. I can make all the connections I need to make from the comfort of my home.

After the list of potential podcasts and telesummits is compiled, I can start reaching out to the hosts or the booking managers. I can get over the hurdle of not having an established reputation by offering the host or booking manager a free session to demonstrate how quickly I can help them improve their lives with energy work. I let the instant shifts and positive outcomes speak for themselves. Now that the hosts and booking managers can personally attest to the energy work, everyone is aligned with the same goal to work together to allow my message to be shared, to be in service to as many people as possible. The hosts and booking managers become highly interested and motivated in booking me for their podcasts and telesummits as soon as possible, as they understand the incredible life-changing value I am able to introduce to their listeners.

My next step is to come up with a product or service to offer to the audience that is in alignment with what areas they feel like they need extra help in. Research has shown that the customers of podcasts and telesummits prefer digital audio recordings to many other forms of media. I decide to create a series of audio recordings on the topic of abundance, as helping people achieve more abundance really lights me up inside and fulfills me on a deep level. As a bonus, it is also possible for me to take the transcripts from the audio recordings and turn them into a book or a companion guide.

Depending on the format of the podcast or telesummit, it is customary to give a free gift to the audience to help establish trust. A book would work well here. I could easily turn my autobiography into a lead magnet or create a guided journal or workbook that complements whatever product or service I am offering during the interview. Even if a listener receives the free book but doesn't purchase a product or service from me initially, it plants a seed of trust and goodwill that the person will remember when they are in need of a talented energy healer.

During the interview, I get to share my story and my message while showcasing my unique skills to thousands of people at once. I get to give demonstrations to prove how effective working with me for a few minutes can be to make my offering as irresistible as possible. Because I also built rapport with the host before my interview with the free session, the host is able to share his or her personal testimonial during the interview to create more trust in my products and services.

I can easily expect to expand my client base by the hundreds or higher from each interview. With the newly established client base, I can use my mailing list to offer more life-changing products and services. How does it get any better than that?

You can reach Vera at veramirna.com.

20

MONETIZE YOUR KNOWLEDGE BY ANITA PLAK SEMPRIMOZNIK

What is your business?

I help people discover ways to monetize their knowledge and create the lifestyle business they're passionate about.

My decades of business experience and innate ability to think strategically allow me to see the big picture—to visualize outcomes and results. I then lay out a roadmap and a proven process for my clients to follow to ensure they achieve success.

I also play a key role in helping clients plan and implement multi-channel marketing strategies for their brands.

What have been the key factors to your success and why?

The key factors to my success are a combination of strategic approach, determination, lifelong learning, adapting to the trends, sticking to my values, and being brave enough to make tough decisions. Fortunately,

I have an innate ability to think strategically, to connect the dots, and to sense or feel where the trends are heading in my line of business.

I have had my own successful business for several years now. Today, it looks quite different than in the early days, in 2007, when I opened it. Since then, my business evolved and continues to evolve in a way that supports my goals and desired lifestyle.

Previously, I worked for several years in a corporate management position, so I knew exactly how to run a successful company. However, just before I opened my own company, I was on a path to burnout. Therefore, my goal back then was to open my own business that would enable me to have a balance between my business and personal life, and that I follow my passion of helping people by sharing my knowledge.

Most people were surprised when I announced that. As the majority of those I spoke with believed that you need to work harder as an entrepreneur, and that you have no private life. Yes, in a way, it is harder. But not harder from a working-hours perspective. It's harder because you suddenly get a lot of pressure when striving to make a sound foundation for the future. All the while working in the business to earn a decent income and make clients happy. You need to be constantly aware of where you're heading, knowing your why, and you work *on* the business, not just *in* the business. That's the hard part. The rest is fun and fulfilling.

I know many entrepreneurs who work long hours and never have time for their families. I believe this is their personal choice, not the situation they're forced into. There are, of course, some exceptions.

I believe we need to be conscious of it at all times. It is easy to fall into the trap of getting caught up in your clients' never-ending cycle of demands and seemingly urgent matters. They always need you, there is always something urgent, there is always someone who missed a deadline, and it has an effect on you whether you like it or not. We may suddenly realize that we're spinning in the hamster wheel. However, it is solely our decision whether we allow it to affect us and how to manage it.

This is something I have experienced and corrected several times in the past. It is extremely hard, and it takes a lot of courage to make it right. However, every time I look back, I know I have made the right decision, even though it didn't seem that way at the time.

When I figured out that certain repetitive situations were dragging me away from my set direction and putting a lot of stress on me, I decided to make a few changes in my business. Sometimes it also meant I had to let go of some clients who were not the right fit for my business. And those who crossed the line and did not respect my values.

I took action, learned the lesson, and moved on.

Knowing your "WHY" is important. One of the reasons I decided to have my own business was to work less, not more. By being organized, productive, and knowing what I'd like to achieve, that was no problem for me.

Of course, when I look back, the idea of serving people sharing my knowledge was slightly different than the one I strive for today. And that's okay.

I have, since then, evolved as a person, and so has my business. I always knew what I wanted in terms of what kind of lifestyle I desire and what is important to me. Therefore, I have made several adaptations in my business in order to support my goals and desired lifestyle.

I never wanted to create a job just for me. Instead, I'm creating a lifestyle business for me and my family on my terms while creating a legacy by sharing my knowledge.

So, how do I manage to continue to grow and be successful?

- Living and staying tuned to my values.
- I don't judge people. I treat them all with respect.
- Ongoing learning. I always strive to learn from the best. I spend a lot of money every year on training and attending live events or conferences in order to stay on the edge with the latest trends in my line of business.
- I learn from everyday work with my clients. And the more I learn, the more I understand my added value, who I'd like to work with, who I don't want to work with, my preferred way of serving clients, and I'm able to "fine-tune" my business model on the path that is in line with my lifestyle goals.
- I learn from people and situations.
- I learn from people I meet, whether they are entrepreneurs or not. There is always something to learn from everyone. Believe it or not, this is how we grow and evolve.
- I also learn from those who failed. Why, you may ask?

I try to understand why they have failed and reflect it on my situation so that I don't make the same mistake. And by this, I'm not just thinking about the business scenarios. I also evaluate personal touch, behavior, and communication.

- Part of my ongoing learning is also reading. I read a lot. Mostly non-fiction about topics I'm passionate about and personal development.
- Continuously adapting my business model to support my mission and desired lifestyle.

- Taking the time to work solely *on* the business. Not just *in* the business.
- Investing in working with mentors who can help me take the shortcuts to get results faster.
- Look over the border and find feasible ways to follow my passion and desired business model. Living in a small country makes you think harder.

What is an unusual habit you have as an entrepreneur, and how does it help you persevere?

I can not say this is unusual; however, these are my "specialties" that help me stay on the edge and persevere.

- Explore and research. Always striving to connect the dots to see the big picture.
- I learn from people and situations. Always. From all kinds of situations, whether business or personal.
- I intentionally set time to work *on* the business, not just *in* the business. This gives me time to think, reflect, adapt, and strategize.
- I invest in knowledge and mentorship.
- I use mind-mapping techniques and sticker notes. Sketchnotes are also fun.
- Taking a brainstorming approach for every project or initiative. Even when I need to do a presentation or course, my starting point is brainstorming ideas using mind-maps.
- Always striving for a better process or better, more efficient ways to accomplish the desired outcome.

How have you used a book for your business?

There are many ways we can use books in our businesses. I use mine based on what I'm trying to accomplish in my business at that exact moment or in the future. Each of my books may have a different role in my business.

For example, I have used my books for several different purposes:

- To help my readers solve their challenges or to get better at something they desire to get better at.
- To enable my potential clients to get to know and trust me.
- To educate people about my topic or area of expertise.
- To increase my authority and credibility, showing my expertise.
- To attract new business alliances and collaborators in the online space.
- To set evergreen lead generation on autopilot.
- To strengthen my author profile on Amazon in order to achieve better ranking.
- To create a passive income revenue stream for my business.
- To create a legacy.
- For a good cause: donation to charity.

How I am using them?

- I give away my books instead of business cards.
- I use books when I lecture or keynote. People love this.
- I'm using my author profile link in my email signature.
- I use books as lead magnets for building my email list.
- I give some of them away as gifts.

How do you make money from your books? How do you ensure this will continue to happen? *

Making money using books is a bit complex to answer in a few words. It is your decision before you start writing the book to decide on your intention. What will you use your book for? What's the purpose of having a book?

It is not just about making money from selling your book. It is about what the book does for your business—how much new business you generate by having it.

It's the ripple effect of having a book that counts.

When it comes to writing a book, a lot of people start with the topic they're passionate about or that's dear to their hearts. However, those who intend to make a business around that passion are absolute winners.

And why do I believe that?

I have several books, all best sellers as I write this. All of them are written for a different reason and purpose. And all of them are helping me in one way or another.

- I'm getting new leads for my services and online programs.
- I'm getting new clients based on my books.
- My email list is growing. This gives me the opportunity to build relationships with people and having a "sales machine" on autopilot.
- My passive income revenue stream is strengthening.
- Having books allows me to build alliances with people who are going to promote my programs and services.
- Some of my books are, and some that I plan to write will be,

positioned in a way that will lead readers to the next step: toward my other books, services, or online programs.

And after all, having more books with a best-seller status means—apart from all I have just summarized—I'm setting the foundation for a better ranking on Amazon for my new books that are due to be launched. So, do you see? There is more than just one side of the story.

How can I ensure making money from my books will continue to happen?

Well, the answer is simple. I strategically think about how to plan and evolve my business. I have a clear vision in my mind. I then strategically position each book (whether existing or new) to serve the purpose and to accomplish my goals.

If done right, having a book is a goldmine for your business. Remember, it's about the ripple effect.

What bad advice do you often hear on the subject of authorship or writing a book for your business?

I often hear something in the line of:

You don't need a book.

Or...

Don't waste time writing a book.

Or...

You won't make any money writing books.

And instead...

Do this first: There are other things that are more important.

There are other more effective ways to get leads.

That form of marketing is more effective.

Who are you to write a book? You're not a professional writer.

Writing a book is hard. Take an easier route.

And so on.

People often give advice based on their preferences and what they think, even though they might not have knowledge about this particular topic.

So, what can I answer? Simply, I disagree with such advice. If nothing else, just take all of us—the co-authors of this book—as examples and proven facts for how having a book can be extremely important and profitable in the long run.

If you lost everything—your book, your list, your products, your platform, your fame—and nobody knew who you were, what would you do in the next 30 days to get back on track, and what role would a book or publication take in the process?

This is a good question we should ask ourselves more often. Especially at times when we get overwhelmed by many tactics or shiny programs. Or when we are at a crossroads, trying to figure out which way to turn.

Fact is, you may lose everything, but no one can take your knowledge from you.

What I'd do would depend on the situation. For example, if I just needed to survive or quickly generate the money in order to be able to work on the business, then I'd take Option One.

However, if I just wanted to start from scratch, and income is not a burning issue at that point, then I'd take Option Two.

Option One:

My main goal would be to create something simple and easy to implement fast. I would:

- Write down what I'm good at and how I can help someone solve their problem or help him/her achieve a dream.
- Then brainstorm ideas using the mind-mapping technique.
- Prepare a checklist or simple ebook around those ideas—this would be a lead magnet.
- Record a short training video or educational webinar with a workbook—this would be my first low- to mid-tier product to sell.
- Create a simple funnel that would enable me to make money while building an email list.

Option Two:

My goal would be to set the sound foundation for a successful business in the long run.

First, I would decide what kind of lifestyle I'd like to create, who I can help, and who I want to work with.

Then I'd come up with the ideas for how I can help those I want to work with. What's important to them and what is their path they need to take in order to get the transformation they seek? And what are the roadblocks on their paths that I can help them overcome?

Next would be to brainstorm different ideas, come up with the best scenario, and finalize the idea to write a book, series of books, or multi-author book that will enable me to get leads on autopilot while creating an online course that would lead to the next step, maybe a monthly subscription or high-end program.

Then I'd lay out an exact roadmap of how I'm going to get there.

Part of the roadmap, in the first phase, would be to set up with a simple funnel that enables me to make money while building an email list.

You can reach Anita at anita-ps.com.

21

ARE YOU COMMITTED TO DO THE WORK?
BY MARC REKLAU

What have been the key factors to your success and why?

I put myself out there, and for the first half a year, nothing happened. I kept studying self-publishing, kept studying marketing, and then I got a BookBub deal and that put me right up there in the best-seller charts of Amazon. I had like 40,000 free downloads in a couple days. From then on, I hit a rhythm. I had like one one book per year. I wrote my books, I got two more BookBub deals. I thought it would go on like this forever.

And then they stopped. My sales were dropping, and then last year or one and a half years ago, they dropped even more. That organic visibility was going away a little bit. Many other authors I talked to also notice the same. I was at a point when I was so desperate—when I was losing 1,000 bucks every month—I said, okay, what are the successful authors on Amazon doing? I bought a couple courses and I saw, okay, they had more books—like 20, 30 books—and they always had a book on promotion for $0.99 or free to bring in new readers.

They were really investing a huge amount of money, maybe 30 percent to 50 percent of their monthly sales where invested in ads. I bought Mark Dawson's course, I applied his teachings, and suddenly noticed from July when I started with ads, every month I got like $500 more, and it didn't stop. Whenever I publish a new book, it is like another step on the scale. I can really see it every time.

I try to publish a new book every two or three months. That's what I did for 13 months, and that was what multiplied my income by eight. I now concentrate 80 percent of my time in my books, which means writing more books and promoting books.

Now traditionally published authors of Spain are coming to me and want help with their books.

Sixty percent of the time I focus on ads is just watching the numbers. What am I spending? What am I earning. I watch all my ads. I have lots, like 400 ads. I'm watching things like which keywords get a lot of clicks, which ones sell.

That's the only thing I'm doing every day, and it just took an hour a day for a year. Now it's two hours, but I check the ads every two to three days now. And I keep on learning. I'm now reading a book on Amazon ads, but I am like a typical, old-school guy. When something works, I have a hard time changing it.

Another thing—it's incredible when you look into the psychology of colors. You have red; that is passion. Yellow is a little bit more like tranquility. And then orange, my company color. Transmits, enthusiasm, optimism—spiritualism, even. Look, the Dalai Lama walks around in orange. One designer told me orange means "cheap but good." ING direct is one of the huge banks, cheap but good. Or in Europe we have easyJet, which is a good airline, but a cheap airline. I thought, well, with my books, that kind of fits. My book is cheap—$4.99—but good. It's incredible what our subconscious does.

What is an unusual habit you have as an entrepreneur, and how does it help you persevere?

Oh, I don't think I have unusual habits, but I do have habits that work, like getting up early. Also, I really embrace the idea of consistent, small wins. In my book I see that most reflected in numbers, but you could see that in weight loss, in anything you do.

Sometimes it's better to do something for ten minutes a day for a year, than two hours a day for a month. It sounds easy, but the thing is, we always want to see results quickly. That for me gives courage and confidence to do other things based on that idea, because everybody writes about it and talks about it, and it's just so difficult. But if you try it, and really do it, it's awesome, and that's what I try to tell people.

Careful now. I have written a book called *30 Days*, which promises a life change in 30 days. Thing is, maybe you need 60 or 90 days. Give yourself time, whatever you're doing. The idea is if you can just get 30 days of it done, your subconscious picks it up, and it gets easier, and in the best case, automatic. You know, I noticed I wrote down my affirmations three years ago and my affirmation was always "I earn $5,000 a month easily and effortlessly." I forgot about that. And now I'm earning more than that easily and effortlessly. At the time I wrote it, I couldn't even imagine it, but it happened. Same thing with my goals. I wrote down my ten-year goals seven years ago. I saw my notes some time ago and—WOW—I reached 80 percent of those goals, and I'm sure I'll reach the other 20 percent in the next three years—or quicker. I forgot about this paper for the whole time. It was really magical to see how stuff works.

How do you make money from your books? How do you ensure this will continue to happen?

Mainly through Amazon ads. I had a some success with BookBub Ads. But most of my book sales come from Amazon Ads. In Spain, I'm in a test group, and it's just incredible. The ROI you get in Spain is amazing. Spain is a very small market. The clicks are so much cheaper, between two and five cents.

In Spain, I don't even check my ads because clicks are so cheap. You can even have a hundred clicks for a sale. It's two dollars. Still making a profit. I also don't launch at 99 cents anymore, in Spain. I launch at $2.99, and it works. I put the book on pre-order for six weeks at $2.99, run some ads to it, and write an email to my list every week to remind them that soon the price will go up to $4.99.

Another important factor for me is also that I don't look so much at my ranking anymore. I noticed, for example, when I did the 99-cent launches, my rank was great, but I didn't earn a lot of money. If I sell 20 books at 99 cents, I earn seven dollars. When I sell four $4.99 books a day, I earn $13.97. That's nearly double. I might not have a great rank, but I'm earning double the money.

Multiply this by ten books, and it makes quite a difference in your earnings. I was number one for so long in Spain and also in a top position in the U.S., yet I was losing money because of the price of the book.

Now I'm in five markets. The U.S. like always, Germany, the U.K., Canada, and Spain. In Germany right now I'm earning more money with my English books than with my one German book. That's something I never expected. Same thing in Spain. I'm now promoting my English and German books in Spain and also earn some money. It all adds up. Spain has around 200,000 or 300,000 English-speaking residents. In Germany, I think they have 2 million English speakers, maybe 3 million. It's also our second language, so try promoting your books in these countries. You might have a pleasant surprise. You're exposed to these different markets much more, being in Europe.

My profits come from the U.S. (35percent), Spain (35 percent), Germany (10 percent), UK (10 percent), and Canada (10 percent).

I never had success writing in German because I write "way too happy." It seems they don't like it when you write it that way. At least when you are German. My writing is very American.

If you lost everything—your book, your list, your products, your platform, your fame—and nobody knew who you were, what would you do in the next 30 days to get back on track, and what role would a book or publication take in the process?

I have still my book files, right? I would just upload everything and run ads again. I think anybody can duplicate my success if they work as hard as I did, and they could even do it faster.

A friend of mine multiplied his royalties by eight times in seven months. It took me thirteen months. How did he do it? I guess he worked two or three hours a day on his ads instead of only one hour like me.

Normally I would build up ads very slowly; ten, then another ten, and another ten, and but now when you say everything is gone except my knowledge, I would run 200 or 300 ads on the first day. I would need a little bit of money to play with. Sometimes it takes a while until you are earning money; in the worst case, it takes a hundred clicks for every book to make a sale. But usually it's not like that.

Would I start in Germany or Spain first? Yes, probably, because clicks are a lot cheaper than in the U.S. Running Amazon ads in Spain is really amazing. On the other hand, it was great to learn in the U.S. because it's by far the most competitive market. If you can break even or even make a profit in the U.S., you will definitely make a profit in the U.K., in Germany, or in Spain. You can start really anywhere, anytime.

One thing, though. Many writers want to outsource their ads. And that's okay. But have one thing in mind: If you want the maximum profit, you better do your ads yourself. Nobody will do your ads as well as you. Nobody. I also noticed that all the authors I know that are really earning some money ($10,000 and more per month) do their own ads. So there must be something to it.

In my workshops, I tell people: "Look, 13 months, one hour a day working on my ads, I went from earning $1,000 a month, to earning over $8,000 a month. If you are not ready to commit to working one hour a day on your own ads for thirteen months, then you simply don't deserve to earn that kind of money as a writer. Period."

It sounds harsh, but that's the way it is. Everybody wants to earn $10,000 a month, few want to do the work. Amazon Ads makes it possible. Are you committed to doing the work?

You can reach Marc at marcreklau.com.

22

BECOME A TOP PERSON OF INFLUENCE BY AGUSTIN RUBINI

What is your business?

I have two businesses. I founded FSPal, an award-winning financial technology firm specialized in high impact training, strategic consulting, research, and coaching in financial services for companies that are based around the globe, but mostly in Europe.

I also lead Promoteyourbook.com, an online agency for Amazon advertising, where authors are offered a done-for-them service to optimize book listing and advertising campaigns to maximize book sales.

I am passionate about the potential of books and publishing. There are so many opportunities for being creative and making new products that help people and create value.

What have been the key factors to your success and why?

Timing has been quite an important factor, and I have managed to find profitable areas of business, which were growing, and act on them.

More importantly, I discovered my skills early on. I have a lot of creativity. As a little boy growing up in Argentina, I wanted to be an inventor, and do something around computers. When you know what you want to work on, everything flows.

There are different ways to create wealth. I recommend you choose the one that is aligned with your skills, preferences, and desires. The main wealth-creator archetypes are: creator, mechanic, star, supporter, deal maker, trader, accumulator, and lord.

I see myself as a creator; a person that likes to work on profitable ideas and businesses. I feel okay delegating other activities in my business to other talented individuals. I advise people to look at what their main preference for generating wealth is, then link up with people that have other strengths to complement each other.

Let's cover the other archetypes. Mechanics, like Henry Ford, are not so much into creativity, but they are great at perfecting processes and products. Stars are magnetic people like Oprah Winfrey who can sell anything to anyone. Supporters are great networkers with lots of energy and enthusiasm. Deal makers are great at making ends meet and finding opportunities that are win-win for multiple parties. Traders are people that know how to buy cheap and sell at a high price. They get a kick out of finding bargains. Accumulators are patient and disciplined people that like to grow their wealth steadily. Lords are people that base themselves on a high level of control of fixed assets.

Just to summarize what I have covered, pause for a second and ask yourself, what are your key strengths? Can you identify with any of the archetypes of wealth? Then link up with others to cover the aspects of business that you are not so happy or comfortable doing. It will make you both more productive and happy.

What is an unusual habit you have as an entrepreneur, and how does it help you persevere?

One of the most unconventional habits I rely on is smart corner cutting. Everybody says that you should not cut corners, but what they really mean is to make sure that you are not compromising on quality.

I think it is really important to figure out a way to improve on your successes in order to be able to repeat them in a faster, easier, and cheaper way.

When we created the advertising service for Promoteyourbook.com, we realized that in order to service a client, we needed to spend about four to six hours of manual work per month. When we broke down where our employees were spending their time, we realized more than half of the time was spent in non-value-adding activities. This was an opportunity for improvement.

We hired an automation guru to produce automation scripts so we could cut time spent on admin activities. We managed to cut these activities in half in little time. Following that, we looked at how we could apply artificial intelligence to get even better results. We realized that by utilizing AI, we could improve results for customers and, at the same time, cut manual work required even more. Our staff now focuses only on value-added activities.

How have you used a book for your business?

The book industry is fascinating, especially the Amazon marketplace. It provides authors with an audience of two hundred million people to look at what you have on offer.

I have used books in many ways. My first book was actually a novel about my experiences as an expatriate living in London, in the United Kingdom. An unexpected result was selling quite a lot of copies, and making a nice stream of passive income.

This then led me into the nonfiction field, where publishing books has helped me raise my profile as one of the leading experts in the field. I have used my books to leverage my influencer profile in financial services. I am surprised by how many executives in Fortune 500 companies buy my books in order to transform their startups and corporations. I also get a lot of interest from universities using my books for their courses. By selling my books, I get the opportunity to share my ideas with influential people in business, frequently at the CXO level. Books are my best allies. They showcase my ideas and what I can do for clients. This results in extra business for my firm, as people will want to hire us to speak at conferences, train their teams, coach their executives, and research specific topics.

There are millions of books out there, so when you become an author, you need to be ready to do the hard work of promoting. This might mean spending time marketing and launching your books. You can also hand off this responsibility to specialists that can do this better than you. By noticing that a lot of authors wanted to focus on writing, I decided to create a done-for-you service to help authors promote their books. It was quite a learning curve to identify all the factors that influence sales of online books, but very rewarding, as the market for indie publishing is massive.

How do you make money from your books? How do you ensure this will continue to happen?

By writing specialized nonfiction books, there is an opportunity to charge an amount that can make significant passive income—even allow you to retire. This is working very well. My advice in this area is to keep updating your books so that they remain current and better than your competitors' books. Also, keep publishing. One book per year would be a good target. Find out about the future of your area, look at how technology changes things, look at what other people are saying. Create a variety of different books around the topic where your passion lies.

And always remember that the bigger opportunity is to create a product ecosystem, where your book is just the first step, your business card. Create online courses, audiobooks, coaching programs, consulting opportunities, virtual seminars, retreats, workshops—this is a very profitable way to build a business.

What bad advice do you often hear on the subject of authorship or writing a book for your business?

Many experts suggest sitting in front of a keyboard and typing x number of words per day, then a book will be born. However, I think people are rushed into writing when they might not have a clear idea on what they want to write about, or how they want to position themselves.

I am more of the idea of creating a book structure to plan your book in a top-down approach. First, try to explain what your book is about in just one sentence. Expand this into a series of ideas that could become your chapters, and follow up by dividing the chapters into subsections.

After creating the structure, sell it to your friends and colleagues and check with them about whether the ideas make sense. Check out what's out there, other books that are published on the topic. Who is writing about this online? Don't rush the writing too much; expand your mind before you start writing and you will produce a book and a set of ideas that will differentiate you and will help you grow your business.

When creating Fintech in a Flash, I realized that I must have read over 5,000 articles on different topics to make sure that I understood what I was talking about. I'm subscribed to 10 different daily newsletters, which allowed me to follow what is happening in the industry, so that I know where things are headed and I can help my clients set a direction for their businesses.

If you lost everything—your book, your list, your products, your platform, your fame—and nobody knew who you were, what would you do in the next 30 days to get back on track, and what role would a book or publication take in the process?

Losing everything can be a blessing in disguise, an opportunity to ask yourself whether you were doing the right things, and whether there is a better way to achieve what you want. I've heard many stories from friends on how they were fired from a job, only to find another one a few weeks later, in which they were paid more and were more excited about their role.

The most important thing that we have is our knowledge, skills, and experience. Look at Donald Trump. He has gone bankrupt several times and still he has come back to become a billionaire. He has used his name and image to get loans and turn around struggling businesses.

I personally like to work inside one industry and become influential in it. If I lost everything I had, I would aim to become a top person of influence inside my chosen industry.

In order to do this, I would spend time developing my pitch, creating published materials, developing a product ecosystem, creating an online profile, and developing partnerships. To make this a bit more real, let's suppose that I am interested in becoming an influencer around crowdfunding, the practice of funding a project or venture by raising money from a large number of people who each contribute a relatively small amount, typically via the internet.

First, I would look at my pitch. When creating my pitch, I want to make sure I know my exact niche. I would answer, with laser focus, the question, "What do I do?"

I would look at influencers and enroll people into my world. What brand essence do I want to convey? Does my message inspire people and leave them wanting to buy products and work with me long-term?

Second, I would consider publishing content. Publishing is really important to position yourself as a credible authority. It creates owner-ship of your chosen micro-niche and puts your name on your work. It also allows you to get a steady flow of high-quality, inbound traffic for free. It is fundamental to create a website and some blog posts expressing your views. Today it is inexpensive to create beautiful websites and reports and make them available globally. I would aim to write five articles on different aspects of crowdfunding where I can showcase my experience and how I deal with challenges. Writing also sharpens communication skills and helps develop a stance on different topics, so make sure you do some of this.

It is not necessary to write a book, but I really like to. As you will be pressed with time, you might consider hiring freelancers to help you create your content. I suggest employing people to help do the research for your topics. It is fundamental that you become the editor of the piece. You need to own your content. When choosing a type of book you want to write, there are different styles you could follow. Books can be a thought leadership book where you convey your ideas (like when I created Fintech in a Flash), it could be a book of interviews (like my book *Fintech Founders*), or simpler books, such as a book of tips or a photo book. Each of these position you in a different way, as somebody that is an expert, or somebody that is well connected. Ideally, have in mind writing different books, and building a book pipeline. In order to start something fast in crowdfunding, I would personally go with a thought leadership book, as I could create it quickly as I master the topic.

Third, I would create my product offering. There is no point in having an audience if you have nothing to offer them. Having products is key to growing a business. Many small businesses focus on exchanging time for money. One of the fastest ways to grow your business quickly is to move beyond thinking about products and services, and begin to develop a product ecosystem. Productizing your services allows you to build business assets that generate revenue on your behalf. For my example on crowdfunding, I would start with offering a couple companies a strategy masterclass for free, which I would record and offer as a free product to other potential clients. Every business should have at least one free product, an information product that educates people as to why they should do business with you.

Having experience in doing masterclasses, it would take me just one day to organize and execute this session. In addition to this, I would offer a face-to-face training to one company interested in crowdfunding, which would be recorded for a group. I would then get a freelancer to edit the videos and produce an online course for me. This can be achieved in a couple of weeks.

Fourth, I would elevate my profile. You need to stand out on the internet. When people google you, they need to see videos, photos, articles of you. You are who Google says you are. When building a profile online, I'm looking for generating leads and enquiries, converting leads and enquiries into sales more frequently, increasing the average spend of my customers, increasing the frequency of purchasing, and improving my overall brand.

So for my crowdfunding expert example, I would make sure that my profile is spotless on LinkedIn. I would connect with key influencers that I find in that segment. I would work with social media specialists to build content for this network as well as for Twitter and Instagram. I would also look at getting my profile into business websites, such as Crunchbase and PitchBook, where executives look for people.

Finally, I would look at setting up partnerships with other businesses and influencers in the niche I am aiming at. Your real wealth comes when you leverage your existing value with others. A great partnership can take your business to the next level.

To get started, create a pitch on how you work together with others. As you will only be starting, try to offer value in your product and affiliate incomes to others for promoting your services. Once you have built up a list, you will be able to organize things together, such as virtual summits.

The road to success can be a long one; however, one month is enough to plant your flag and start getting traction on the road of profitability. Ensure you choose a topic that you enjoy.

You can reach Agustin at promoteyourbook.co.

23

USE YOUR STORY BY JAMES B ARCHER JR

What is your business?

The ShareLingo Project is a social enterprise that helps English and Spanish speakers meet and practice together. This program has helped thousands of individuals, as well as schools, non-profits, and corporations where the two cultures connect. ShareLingo is dedicated to breaking down cultural barriers through a proprietary language-exchange model developed by the founder.

What have been the key factors to your success and why?

Tenacity—and the core belief that the world needs what I am providing.

What is an unusual habit you have as an entrepreneur, and how does it help you persevere?

This is not my first start-up. In every case, it has been like raising a child—requiring long hours and commitment, as well as many sacrifices. People around me constantly tell me that I work too hard, I need a break, I'm killing myself. These are often the same people that see the rewards later on, and say, "He's so lucky."

I don't think my habits are unusual for an entrepreneur. I try to get enough sleep, and I get up early every morning and get excited about the day ahead. I pick ONE thing and try to get that thing done as early as possible because the rest of the day will inevitably be a train wreck. The idea is to keep moving forward and not move backward.

How have you used a book for your business?

My books do not generate a lot of royalties—and any profits go to charity anyway—so they don't contribute to my business bottom line. But that was never the intention. My first book, *Beyond Words*, was written for credibility (and to share my passion for cultural exchange with the world).

What bad advice do you often hear on the subject of authorship or writing a book for your business?

1. USE A PUBLISHER! I would *never* do anything but self-publish.
2. Launch first. During a launch, you want to convey authority —that is, that you know what you are talking about. One of

the greatest methods of creating authority is to have a best-selling book before the launch.

If you lost everything—your book, your list, your products, your platform, your fame—and nobody knew who you were, what would you do in the next 30 days to get back on track, and what role would a book or publication take in the process?

When I started The ShareLingo Project, this was almost the case. I don't mean that I had lost all of those things—my list, product, platform—but in this case, the new project didn't have anything to do with my previous endeavor. So I was starting from scratch.

Here's the thing: One does not lose the knowledge and experience one has gained. I used the experience I acquired, and the connections I have made along this journey of mine, to reach out and start sharing that knowledge with as many people as possible. Of course, this included blogs, Facebook, YouTube, and other avenues. But I believe that sharing your knowledge through the vehicle of a published best-selling book is one of the best ways to begin the process.

When I started ShareLingo, I needed to reach out to the media and other influencers. Let me give two examples. First, I wanted to get some exposure on TV about my mission and goals. I shared a copy of my book with the CEO of Telemundo here in Denver, and he liked my message about connecting cultures enough to ask one of his reporters to do a piece on it. If I had pitched the reporter directly, saying I have a great new idea for language learning, it *may* have gotten her attention, or not. But when the CEO asked her to do a piece about ShareLingo, she really took interest.

Another goal I had was to connect with local government. By sharing the book, I was able to get the support of the number one person in the Office of Immigrant Integration. As you can imagine, he's very well connected in exactly the space I wanted to be in. As you can also imagine, he's unbelievably busy and difficult to reach. But because of the message in my book, and the authority it provided, he immediately started thinking not only about how his office could help with the project, but also about who else he could connect me with. And then *those* people could also read the book in order to understand my message and mission. And many of those people became advocates of the project as well.

If that's not enough, there's one other "authority" aspect of the book I want to mention.

My current focus is with *online* marketing of my course and membership to help English and Spanish speakers find each other and practice together. I believe this model helps me serve the most people. And I needed to get the message out to the masses that they have a new way to learn a language—and it's based on human beings, not apps and computers.

Since ShareLingo started as a local project here in Denver, people in other cities and other countries (like Guatemala, Colombia, Nicaragua, Cuba, etc.) have no idea who I am or whether I know what I'm talking about. But when I introduce myself in many of my main marketing and training videos, I am able to tell people that I'm a "Best-selling author" and share a link to the book on Amazon, where they can read the reviews and possibly even order a copy for themselves. More importantly, I'm able to instantly convey to my online audience that I have the knowledge that can help them. Showing them my book, with its "best-seller" badge, is vastly quicker and more powerful than me simply telling them I've helped thousands of people do what they want to do. (Of course, I tell them that also...).

Now, here's what I recommend *you* do:

Outline your "story"—about how you personally got started doing what you do and how you gained your experience. Record a video of that story—it doesn't matter if anyone will ever see the video, so don't stress about the production quality.

Then, outline what you would do if you were to make a course teaching what you know to other people. How you would lead them step by step to achieve the results you can help them with. Don't over-think it. Your goal here is to simply help people. Think of it like if you were doing a free Saturday course for the Rotary Club. Record those modules as videos also.

Get all the videos transcribed into text—there are very inexpensive services that do that, like Rev.com.

Turn that text into a book. You will see how it naturally falls into chapters and content. That's going to give you something you can turn into a best-selling book.

It's a much simpler process than most people think. Certainly much simpler than I thought when I started my first book.

One other thing before I go—think about interviewing people in your industry about your topic and then using those interviews in your book also. That's one way to get people interested in you before the book is launched. It's also an easy way to add interesting content to your book if you don't feel like it has enough.

Enjoy the process! Ciao for now.

You can reach James at archer.com.

24

BE OF SERVICE BY LORI SAITZ

What is your business?

I work with two groups of people:

1. I help managers ensure their employees they send to conferences come back with valuable connections that benefit the company. They rely on me to help them create follow-up systems that turn leads from conferences into clients.
2. I help business professionals—such as architects, accountants, attorneys, engineers, and consultants—who want to make partners at their firms and build connections that lead to new business.

What have been the key factors to your success and why?

There are three key factors to my success:

1. Clarity around what problem I solve for clients. It took me a while to understand the real problem for which I have a solution, as well as how to describe the solution in a way that people immediately "get it." Then I had to decide who my ideal client is.

Too often, people say their ideal client is "anyone who..." They think the wider they cast their nets, the easier it will be to find business. In fact, the complete opposite is true. When you are very clear and focused on a precise niche, it's easier to attract clients. People want to work with specialists, not generalists. If you have a heart condition, you want a cardiologist, not a family practice doctor.

Additionally, it's easier for people to send you referrals when you can give them laser focus on who you want. "Anyone who..." and their mind goes blank. For example, by using the description, "Managers who send employees to conferences," I give a clear picture, and people can usually pull up the name of someone they know.

2. Persistence, aka relentlessness. My family would label this trait as stubbornness (haha). The truth is, as a business professional, your resolve will be tested.

You have to develop a determination that will keep you going when everything falls apart. I'm not being negative here—I'm actually one of the most optimistic people around—but at times, business can be difficult. There will be days or weeks or months when everything sucks. You can quit, or you can say, "not today," and keep pushing forward.

3. My incredible network. C'mon, I write and talk about networking all the time, of course, that's going to be a key to my success! In fact, it's the most important one. No matter what you want to accomplish, your network—that collection of people you know through any aspect of life—is what's going to determine if and how quickly you get there. If

you're not getting access to opportunities, it's because your network is not big or strong enough (or possibly not organized well enough for you to tap into it).

Many people think of a network as clients, associates, referral partners, and so on. That's only part of it. Your support network is equally essential. You need those allies who will hold your hand when things aren't going well, cheer you on when you're winning, and kick your butt when you need it.

What is an unusual habit you have as an entrepreneur and how does it help you persevere?

The first is working out. I developed this odd passion for weight training, health, and fitness when I was seventeen. No one else in my family was into this, so I'm not sure where it came from, but it's served me well in staying healthy and sane. The gym is my sanctuary, and I like to go at least four times a week.

The second habit is one I've established more recently. Many successful people practice meditation, and I knew it was beneficial, but I could never get myself to do it consistently. In the past year, I finally committed to meditating every morning before I start my day. It's made a tremendous impact. I'm much more grounded and focused. It's crazy how much synchronicity happens now.

Oh, and thirdly, peanut butter. Crunchy, creamy, doesn't matter. They're both good. That love comes straight from my dad. I don't eat it every day like he does, nor do I pair it in unusual combinations—such as with turkey and cheese. Nonetheless, you will always find a jar of all-natural peanut butter in my pantry.

How have you used a book for your business?

I wrote my first book as a lead magnet. The goal was to share good and valuable information that would help people feel more comfortable networking. I wanted to give them an introduction to who I am and what I know, so as to build my credibility as an expert.

How do you make money from your books? How do you ensure this will continue to happen?

I make very little money from individual book sales. The book is a means of entry to other revenue-generating opportunities, such as speaking engagements, joint projects, and media interviews.

As a professional speaker and workshop leader, a book replaces a business card these days. I ensure the book continues to deliver by talking about it and sharing it with prospective clients. I've also created an audio version of it for those who prefer to listen instead of read (I'm happy to offer my voice-over services to anyone else who'd like an audio version of his or her book).

What bad advice do you often hear on the subject of authorship or writing a book for your business?

Not sure I've heard much bad advice. What I have heard is the belief or idea that writing a book is a long, tedious process that takes an insane amount of time.

It's important to map out what you want to cover, using whatever process works for your brain. For some, that's a traditional outline, and for others, it might be a mind map. Then fill in the details and add the humanizing stories. If you set aside a certain amount of time each day or each week and consistently stick with it, your book will materialize faster and with less struggle than you might expect.

My observation is that the thought of creating an entire book is overwhelming. But when you break it down into smaller, bite-size pieces, it's not as much so.

I look at it like working out. If you're fifty pounds overweight, and you think about how you're going to reduce your weight by the entire fifty pounds and get in shape, it's intimidating to even start. But, if you begin with a plan for just the first six weeks and take it one day at a time, it's much more manageable.

It's the same with writing a book. Create or invest in a plan and follow it. No need to reinvent the wheel.

If you lost everything—your book, your list, your products, your platform, your fame—and nobody knew who you were, what would you do in the next 30 days to get back on track, and what role would a book or publication take in the process?

I've heard this question asked in podcast interviews before, but I've never really thought about what I'd do if this happened to me.

For sure, I'd start with building relationships. I'd move to a city I really liked and start meeting people by going to a variety of business and social events. I'd also start talking to people online, starting with LinkedIn because I find the conversations there more interesting and intelligent than other social media platforms.

In the interest of being of service, I'd figure out the intersection of the most common or pressing challenge facing the people I'm meeting and my natural talents. Again, it would have something to do with building relationships—whether strengthening existing ones with current clients or starting new ones with potential clients.

First, I'd clearly define what problem, challenge, or pain potential clients are feeling. For example, if their client turnover is high, and they're always needing to find new clients to replace the ones they're losing, that's a costly and painful problem.

Then I'd figure out how to convey how what I have to offer can solve their problem. What's the best way to help them see that my expertise and the service or product I have can help them keep clients longer? That's defining the value I deliver.

Next, I'd choose a specific niche. No doubt you've heard this advice before. That's because it has merit. I speak from experience because I did not do this with my first business, and in hindsight, it's very clear I should have. My business would have been far more profitable and succeeded faster had I done that.

Actually, this point reminds me of an interaction I had with a woman at a networking event. I asked her who her ideal client was, and she said, "Anyone with skin." Okaaaaay. That's not very specific. My cat has skin. Would she be a good client for you?

So I'd clearly define who has the problem I want to solve, as well as who I want to work with. If I could solve this problem for ten different kinds of businesses, I'd think about which one or two of those industries I'd have the most fun with. It's my business. I'm not going to choose to work with people who annoy me, or have a reputation of being arrogant, or don't have the money to hire me.

Now that I know what I want to do and for whom, I'd write up my LinkedIn profile to very specifically talk to those people. For example: Helping financial advisors extend the lifetime value of clients through appreciation marketing.

Every day for the next thirty days and beyond, I'd post a variety of content—articles, posts, videos—that incorporated some kind of story and relate it to that problem I solve. The story part of my content is important here because humans have been storytellers for centuries. It's how we've shared culture and documented history forever. People enjoy, respond to, and remember stories.

I want my ideal clients to:

1. See who I am as a person, so they can get to know me.
2. See that I understand their problem and can solve it.

Every piece of content has a call to action. It could be a simple question at the end of my post: "Have you ever had this experience? How did you handle it?"

I might also add, "When you're ready, I can help you keep clients happier for longer. Message me to find out more."

I'm not looking to beat them over the head with a sales pitch or scarcity tactic. My deal is building relationships, which happens through the know, like, and trust process, not high-pressure sales copy.

At the same time I'm posting content, I'm also using LinkedIn Navigator to find people who meet my criteria and connect with them. The more people I'm connected to, the more people will see and interact with my content.

I'm using Navigator because it allows for advanced searches that the free and premium versions don't. I can search based on size of company or seniority within a company. Plus, I'd get an unlimited number of searches, and I can save those searches—"Northern California financial services people," for example.

However, if I didn't have the $90 per month in my budget for Navigator, I'd start with the free version and work within its parameters.

In addition to posting my own content, I'd find other people who are talking to the financial advisors and comment on their content. I'd make sure what I post is relevant and adds value to the discussion. I'm not promoting my services or stealing the spotlight from the original poster.

I am getting my name out there and again building credibility and awareness. Every time I comment somewhere, more people see my name and my headline, which describes what I do and how I help.

People who see that will then look at my profile and want to connect with me.

I don't have any clients yet, so I don't have any testimonials or social proof. In order to get some, I will publicize that I'm taking on five pro-bono clients for a beta program. I'll be very specific about who those five people are. I want advisors who've been in the business for a while, who have an established client base, and who have a good reputation. I also want people who are well-connected because once I do a great job with them, I want them to have a pool of colleagues to whom they can refer me.

I'll let them know that while the program is free, I will expect a video testimonial if—and only if—they feel what I deliver is valuable.

Then I will take them through my program and show them exactly how to use appreciation marketing to extend the lifetime value of their clients. I'll probably even do some of the implementation for them. I want to go above and beyond so they give me glowing recommendations and referrals.

Since I don't have my book, as I'm working with those five clients, I'm documenting what challenges they've been facing and how my system is helping them keep clients longer and leads to them making more money. Their stories, along with the framework of my system, will become my new book.

Once the book is published, I'll use it as a call to action in my continuous posting of content. "When you're ready, check out my new book."

It will make a great tool for helping my ideal clients get to know me and my process even better, so they feel even more comfortable with me before engaging my services.

While it realistically might take more than thirty days to get a full stable of clients, the above steps could all be done within the thirty days and would certainly get me back on track and moving in the right direction.

$\sim$

Lori can be reached at ZenRabbit.com.

25

GIVE VALUE AND FOLLOW UP BY SEAN SUMNER

What is your business?

I am an author, coach, and community manager for Self-Publishing School, an online school that helps authors of all genres learn the process of self-publishing and how to generate ongoing sales. I manage the online mastermind community made up of thousands of authors who are sharing ideas and tips with each other.

I am also a physical therapist and one of the top spine-care professionals, and I specialize in helping people find solutions to chronic back and neck pain.

Over the past five years, I have transitioned much of my time from one-on-one patient care in the clinic to creating online solutions for patients, including books and online courses.

What have been the key factors to your success and why?

As a healthcare professional, much of my life has been devoted to finding individual solutions for patients, whether it is in the hospital or at home. However, the biggest key factor to my success has been the decision to find ways to get my message out to larger audiences, as opposed to one-on-one care, so I can help more than just one person at a time.

This started by accepting speaking opportunities at universities for both physicians and medical students, then transitioned to writing journal articles and textbooks for physical therapists, doctors, and surgeons. Finally, it evolved into writing books and creating courses directly for the general public.

Amazingly, the journal articles and textbooks took ten times longer to get published than my books did. This is why I no longer rely on publishers or journal review committees; by self-publishing, I can get my message out in weeks or months instead of years.

I have now progressed to managing large online mastermind communities and giving weekly webinars to hundreds of people at one time. The content I teach has changed some; instead of teaching people about back pain, I am now teaching authors and entrepreneurs how to spread their messages.

The second key factor to my success has been the amount of time and money I have invested in high-quality online courses and programs to help me further my career. I spend between $10,000 to $12,000 a year on education, with the vast majority of that in the form of online courses and programs. The most influential of those programs is Self-Publishing School, where I learned the best way to write, publish, and market my own book. Initially, I started as a student, but I am now a coach. I help manage their growing community of authors in their online mastermind program.

I learned early on that you tend to get what you pay for in online training, and although there are some good courses on the market at a lower price, the best courses that get the most proven results tend to cost between $3,000 to $10,000. Those are courses that show five to ten times the return in the long run.

The third factor to my success is that I have been able to find high-quality outsourcers to help me create my books; this includes editors, cover designers, formatters, and marketers. When I first started, I felt I needed to do it all myself. I would spend hours at a time trying to learn the art of cover design, and in the end I found I just was not very good at it. My first cover looked like a seven-year-old used a Sharpie to create it.

Now that I have a team of people to do the tasks I am not well suited for, I can better spend my time on what I do best. Finding outsourcers is difficult if you do not have a network of people to ask for references, and that is why I invest so heavily in quality online courses and mastermind communities. They often have a list of talented people they have already vetted for you.

What is an unusual habit you have as an entrepreneur, and how does it help you persevere?

One of the more unusual habits I have as an entrepreneur is to take lessons and motivational strategies I learned from coaching local youth sports and incorporate them into how I work with adult clients and write my books or courses. As an active father of two young daughters, I have always been involved in their after-school activities and sports.

When trying to teach or coach children, you have to build the lesson around something that is fun and engaging or you will quickly lose them. If you apply that same lesson to coaching, teaching, or writing for adults, then they, too, will be more engaged and more likely to get a good result or implement what you are teaching. I find myself studying the best coaches of the local little league teams or kids' soccer camps to see how they use games, prizes, and fun to teach.

How have you used a book for your business?

My books are an integral part of my business, and although they bring in revenue each year directly from book sales, the two ways I use books most in my business are to bring in leads for other products or courses and establish myself as an authority on the topic.

When it comes to bringing in leads, the book is the easiest way for me to find people throughout the world who are interested in my subject. Each week, dozens of new people read my books and learn about me and what I have to teach because they purchased my books on Amazon.

Throughout the ebooks, I have links to additional information that readers can click on to download in exchange for their email or contact information. From there, they are added to an email list, and I follow up with them with information about my online courses or any other product or affiliate offer I have.

Instead of paying Google or Facebook to identify good leads for me to advertise to, by having the book available for purchase on Amazon, people who are actively searching for my topic find me easily.

Establishing myself as an authority is the second way I use books in my business, and there is no better way to establish that position than having a best-selling book on the subject.

When I was focused on building my physical therapy practice, I would often visit doctors in my area to establish a relationship for referrals, and as soon as I showed them that I was a bestselling author on solutions for back and neck pain, I was immediately put on the top of the list. Most of the doctors never even purchase or read the book—just the fact that I have the book, and others have read and reviewed it, is enough for them.

How do you make money from your books? How do you ensure this will continue to happen?

At this point in my author career, I make money from books in several different ways:

1. Direct sales of digital, print, and audio books on Amazon and other book sellers.
2. Online course sales from people who read the book and want to dive deeper into the topic.
3. Consulting clients who want me to help them replicate the success that I had with my own books and courses.

To make sure I continue to make money from the books and get more readers, I focus on three things: Amazon ads, reviews, and making personal connections with influencers.

Amazon ads are the biggest driver of leads to my book, and I highly recommend all authors use them. I target a wide variety of keywords instead of focusing only on the exact keywords that are most relevant to my book, and although this may bring some people who are not really interested in my topic and my click-through rate may be lower, it can also attract people who may have a passing or outside interest in the subject, and then you can let your cover and sales page take them across the finish line.

The result for me is a lower click-through rate but a higher number of overall sales at the end of the month. Although I love the results I get from Amazon ads, I find the process a bit tedious and not my natural talent, so I use a service called BookAds (founder Brian Berni also contributed a chapter to this book) to help me manage and scale my ads. I have also started experimenting with BookBub ads and Facebook ads; however, Amazon ads still have the best return on investment for me by far. The ad gets people to look at my book, but in order to get them to purchase, they need social proof. That is where reviews come in.

Reviews are the biggest reason people purchase my books once they get to the book sales page. I have over 100 reviews with an average of four and a half stars. This presents the potential reader with enough social proof to make a decision to purchase. Most people rely heavily on those reviews, and although most people don't actually read many of the individual reviews, it is still important to see that others have given their blessing to this book. I have found that the minimum number of reviews needed is 20; after that point, most potential readers feel there is enough social proof to trust.

If you do not have at least 20 reviews, then you must focus on getting to that point before driving traffic to your book sales page. In order to keep my reviews going, I actively ask people who read my books to leave a review by following up with an email to anyone who gets a lead magnet within the book and placing a "Review Plea" page at the end.

Finally, to get those people who are not actively looking for a book on Amazon but are still interested in the topic, I focus on creating relationships with other influencers who are also related to the topics I write about. In the case of my books on back and neck pain, I created specific relationships with well-known physicians and surgeons who have endorsed my book. I have also done multiple podcasts and webinars with other groups who have audiences dealing with chronic pain or long-term back issues. To create or build those key relationships with influencers, I rely on personal reach-outs via messenger or email and focus on how I can help them first.

If you are interested in building those types of relationships, I highly recommend a book called *Beyond Influencer Marketing* by my good friend, Cloris Kylie. That is where I learned how to systematize the way I connect with people. She breaks down specific strategies that I continue to use with success today.

What bad advice do you often hear on the subject of authorship or writing a book for your business?

I often hear people talk about the overwhelming importance of the first week of the book launch, and that they should focus all their marketing efforts on getting people to buy the book in the first couple of days, including friends and family.

I have worked with thousands of authors at this point, many of which have launched multiple books, and the truth is that the launch is just one phase of your book—it will not make or break you. The work of promoting your book is done months before, during, and long after the short period that is designated for your launch, and a poor showing at launch just means you need to work harder in the next phase of marketing.

When your book has been on the market for two to three years, you will then realize that what happened during that two-week period at launch meant very little in the grand scheme of things.

That does not mean you should not try to have a good launch. It just means that you should not devote all your time and resources for that small window, and you do not need to call it quits if the launch does not go as well as you expected.

If you lost everything—your book, your list, your products, your platform, your fame—and nobody knew who you were, what would you do in the next 30 days to get back on track, and what role would a book or publication take in the process?

I would focus my first 30 days on researching, marketing, and pre-selling a program that involved a small group of 20 to 30 people in an online course and coaching program followed by a book on the exact same subject matter to get ongoing leads.

This may sound like a backward concept for many, and up until the past few years I would have thought this was completely insane. I could never imagine that someone would pay for something that I have not created yet. As a physical therapist, I was used to seeing the patient first and then billing for it afterward. If you are a teacher, coach, healthcare professional, or work in any other service- or physi-cal-product-based business, then you probably have the same mindset I did. What I have learned is that selling a product before you deliver it is common for all different markets, both online and offline.

If you are having difficulty with this (much like I did at first), try to imagine your clients are paying you as they would pay for college tuition; they pay for your classes at the beginning of the semester, and then throughout the next two to three months, you teach new things week by week until the end of the semester.

I am going to break it down into three ten-day sprints.

The first ten days would be completely focused on research and planning to find the best topic to teach based on my experience and the needs of those I have worked with in the past. It is important to make sure that there is a direct, pressing need for whatever it is I am teaching, so that people are actively looking for a solution within the next 30 days and are willing to pay someone to help them. I would choose a topic that has a clearly defined endpoint and some clear milestones along the way to show progress as we go. Before deciding on a topic, I would make sure I have at least ten different hour-long, one-on-one conversations with potential clients to make sure I have clearly defined their needs.

With my next ten days, I would work to get as many people as I can to register for a webinar or live event on the subject by reaching out to everyone I know via email, social media, and even phone calls to get the word out. I would advertise the webinar as a one-time event where I would teach my top tips for the concept and make sure to inform people it is something I may never do again.

During the webinar, I would go over my top three tips or strategies they can use to be successful right away and then showcase the upcoming course and all the results they can achieve if they join. Then I would offer a one-time, half-hour consultation where we could discuss how to personalize the strategies from the webinar to their specific situation.

The final ten days I would spend following up with everyone who attended the webinar, watched the replay, or even showed any interest in the program, trying to get as many one-on-one phone calls booked as possible. On those calls, I would get to know the person as well as I can, focusing on their problems and goals.

After we go through the content on the call, I would spend an additional fifteen minutes discussing my program and offering them a chance to join. I have found that this approach of getting on the phone with people is by far the best way to get your first 20 to 30 clients, and then you can make the decision in the future as you get more leads if you want to transition to a sales page or continue doing sales over the phone.

Once the class is sold, it is time to transition to building the content from one topic to the next until the students have everything they need to reach the endpoint that was defined at the start.

After delivering the class from beginning to end to the first round of students, I'd then take that content and create a book on the topic. I can use the lessons taught to this first round of people to create the outline for my book.

By waiting until the first round of the course is delivered, you get the chance to adjust and refine your content to include answers to all the additional questions you got from those first students, making it seem like you are reading the minds of your readers.

Here are two specific ways I would use the book to get leads for the future:

1. Within the book, I would create easy transitions for people to learn more about the topic by offering a "lead magnet," then follow up with them via email to discuss the course.

2. I would advertise the book on social media as an inexpensive solution to their problem, then as soon as they purchase I would follow up with them and introduce them to the course as a more comprehensive solution to the problem.

I have found that people who purchase the book are the hottest leads I can get. They have already done most of the work by doing an initial search for answers to find my book, then made the decision that I am an appropriate teacher and that they are willing to make a purchase and spend time learning about the subject from me. At that point, I just need to give great value within the book and follow up with them to offer even more value with the course.

Sean can be reached at seansumner.com.

26

CONNECTION BY RICARDO TEIXEIRA

What is your business?

I have two businesses: I help lawyers to be Elite Lawyers, and I help entrepreneurs to be unstoppable in their businesses using software, consulting, and training that focuses on high performance and digital marketing.

KAMAE is a software company that focuses on selling software solutions, consulting services, and online courses to lawyers to help transform them into Elite Lawyers.

At KAMAE, we have a kickass team, and we are always in Kamae!

So, I focus on two markets:

Lawyers in law firms and small business owners.

I use my Martial Arts knowledge in my company, products, and services.

What have been the key factors to your success and why?

Five Factors: Energy, Mindset, Strategy, Action, and Connection.

Energy: If we don't have the necessary energy to motivate our team, to excite our clients, and to execute, nothing will happen.

Mindset: The life of an entrepreneur is full of ups and downs. We need to have the right mindset to absorb failures as fuel to improve and see problems as challenges, so we can smile and find solutions.

Strategy: We can have all the energy and the right mindset, but if we do the wrong things, at the wrong time, with the wrong people, we will not succeed.

Action: If we have Energy, Mindset, and Strategy, but we don't do shit, nothing will happen. Taking action is necessary!

With these four key factors, we can succeed, but we need the fifth to go far. The fifth is Connection. We must surround ourselves with people who challenge us. Like Jim Rohm said: "We are the average of the five people we hang out the most."

What is an unusual habit you have as an entrepreneur and how does it help you persevere?

One of my unusual habits is that I have is to make KIAI every morning when I'm driving my car.

You have probably seen people "screaming" in martial arts... It's not a scream. It's a physiological movement that changes our mental state, giving the mind energy and emptiness, which is necessary sometimes.

Another unusual habit of mine is: KAIZEN by RT.

KAIZEN means "good change," and in Japan, it's associated with continued improvement. I apply this to myself daily and ask myself three questions:

- What did I do well?
- What should I do differently?
- What can I do tomorrow that I will do better than today?

This helps everyday to be better, evolve, and push me to improve even more.

How have you used a book for your business?

I wrote a book specifically targeted to lawyers. The goal of the book was to attract lawyers to my business.

Now, as I'm writing this, I am signing a deal with a publisher for three books, in the next two years, targeted at entrepreneurs. The book will focus on helping them in their online marketing and their performance so they can reach their goals, while also having an impact on the people around them.

How do you make money from your books? How do you ensure this will continue to happen?

The books don't bring in a significant amount of money; it is what I do inside of the books that creates a strategy. I put calls to action inside of the book, which lead to a funnel where I upsell products. This is a way to leverage the book.

When I write books, I also focus on their being timeless, so I can always push it as a sale, lead magnet, or gift for live events or students in my courses.

What bad advice do you often hear on the subject of authorship or writing a book for your business?

The worst advice that I have ever heard is that you will make money only writing the book. People don't realize that bookstores are full of authors who don't make enough money to live off of. The authors don't know how to monetize.

If you lost everything—your book, your list, your products, your platform, your fame—and nobody knew who you were, what would you do in the next 30 days to get back on track, and what role would a book or publication take in the process?

If I had to start everything from the beginning with no book, no list, no platform, no fame, I would do two things:

1st: I would start my own thing.

2nd: Partner with an expert who already has an audience.

Day 1: Open a Facebook business account and create video content about my goal for the next 30 days. In my video and Facebook Live, I would invite the viewers to see how I'm going to make a comeback. I would also invite them to join my Facebook group.

Day 2: Create an ebook and utilize it as a lead magnet, explaining my 30-day plan. I would do another Facebook Live showing this ebook.

Day 3: Create a funnel for the ebook and start to build an email list. Then another Facebook Live showing the creation of the content.

Day 4: Offer "Quitting is not an Option!" A 30-day challenge to help with the comeback. Facebook Live "I'm thinking of creating this... What do you think?" and get potential clients.

Day 5: Prepare content for a free masterclass (following the Product Launch Formula—PLF—principles for a seed launch). Facebook Live building anticipation that it is coming and offering the ebook. Create the funnel for people to sign-up.

Day 6: Do another Facebook Live announcing the masterclass in 10 days. Go to the store, search for books that are in the top 20, and search the authors that could have a market that complement mine. Email them.

Day 7: Facebook Live. Follow up with the authors by phone

Day 8: Facebook Live. Select the authors that respond and propose a Zoom call for a 50 percent partnership with an irresistible offer.

Day 9: Facebook Live. Draft a plan to work together with the authors.

Day 10-13: Finish the plan: Build the Platforms, Content Plan & Publishing and design the membership plan. Doing Facebook Lives everyday.

Day 14: Present the offer to the author and come up with an offer (membership) based on the content of the book. Establish a deadline that I have until the end of the month to start.

Day 15: Finish content creation with all the feedback from Facebook Lives for the masterclass

Day 16: Masterclass Day (Doing the offer)

Day 17: Email and FB Live

Day 18: Email and FB Live

Day 19: Email and FB Live

Day 20: Second Masterclass Day

Day 21: Email and FB Live

Day 22: FB Live and Close Cart. Challenge starts in nine days.

Day 23: Starting one of the modules for seven days, prepare the challenge to break any limiting beliefs that people have, and continue with the Facebook Lives talking about the challenge for next month.

Day 24: "I'm not good enough."

Day 25: "It's only working for others."

Day 26: "Not in my market."

Day 27: "I don't have the time."

Day 28: "I'm not ready. Need more time."

Day 29: "No excuses."

Day 30: Start Challenge!

In the end, I will have three products: package all Facebook Lives, make a course to sell, and have the author deal as a backup.

27

REVERSE THE PROCESS BY LAURA VAN DEN BERG - SEKAC

What is your business?

I'm a bestselling author and Next Level Mentor.

I work with growth-driven, out-of-the-box thinkers who feel they can create at a higher level, but cannot access it or stay there.

Their struggle is they have so many ideas that they get distracted or paralyzed by too many possibilities. They lose their focus and don't take that next step because they don't know where to start, how to start, or how it could work.

I help them envision their ideas more clearly and transform the blocks that are getting in their way. As a result, they can realize their ideas and reach that next level.

As an author and lifelong explorer of my inner depths, I know how frustrating it is when you cannot get your idea out satisfactorily. I find it very fulfilling to help others so they do not have to go through the same experience.

What have been the key factors to your success and why?

Let's define what success is first. For me, it's accomplishing my goals. However, to call something a success, it must include an element of transformation, and the result must generate more joy, freedom, peace, or clarity.

I look at my business from the financial point of view and from the standpoint of personal fulfillment. Both sides must be in balance. Is my company doing what it's supposed to do, like providing value to my readers and customers? Is it making money?

Besides making money and serving the customers, my work needs to be meaningful and feed my soul and the soul of people I work with. It must help both me and my customers grow as people and enhance the quality of our lives.

I noticed that when life challenges me, it's often because I didn't honor who I truly am. Karma comes back to me in the form of hardship. This lesson taught me to respect my needs and to align everything I do with what matters to me the most.

But I also found out it's not sufficient to honor it. You must bring what matters to you to a higher level all the time.

To prosper, a positive mindset is crucial. That mindset has to be aligned with your core values.

Consequently, my business and personal goals must be in line with my philosophy and thus my values, such as integrity, joy, and personal growth. I want them to be integrated into my way of thinking, my behavior, and the way I treat myself and others.

Honoring my values means being impeccable with my energy in all circumstances. It means keeping my intentions and respecting each other's boundaries. I always ask myself, "Is what I plan to do respectful and loving toward myself? Does it bring me joy? Does it honor the needs of my readers, my business, and relationships? How can I make it even better?"

This is, of course, a lifelong project.

Another key to success is being unafraid to fail or to let go, if necessary. I can be very perseverant, but when something is no longer working or aiding in my growth, I quit. If a situation doesn't support my progress as a person and there's no potential for further advancement, I move on.

It's not giving up. It's letting go of what's not working. I'm not afraid to walk away from a situation and start anew, because I don't consider it to be a failure. For me, it's the end of one learning curve.

When I experience a setback, I have a weird reaction. Instead of feeling like a failure or like I'm out of my depth, it's as if some stronger force takes possession of me. That force doesn't accept drama, obstacles, or difficulties. It doesn't matter if something seems difficult or impossible. When something goes wrong, it energizes and motivates me to overcome it, rather than to feel discouraged. My inner refusal to give away my power to an impossibility is so strong that it often causes a solution to form out of nowhere.

I know I can always start over again and create a new situation that works better for me and others. I learned this, among other things, when I was running a personal development school in the Netherlands.

I loved teaching and developing new methods. People got great results, yet after about seven years, my passion diminished. I lost my motivation, but I couldn't quite put my finger on why my work didn't satisfy me anymore, or exactly what I wanted to do with my life. In the end, I decided to give it up and open myself up to something new.

I finally ended up in France, pursuing writing—an old dream of mine. I admit the writing process challenged my comfort zone and showed me ruthlessly what lived inside me. I discovered, for example, that when my writing involved exploration, I felt energized. But when I played safe instead of experimenting, I tended to procrastinate.

It took a few years before I understood why my old business didn't fulfill me. Just like writing, starting my development school challenged my comfort zone. I loved it because I enjoy discovering the unknown. But when running the school became a routine, my innate curiosity and need for expansion weren't being satisfied enough.

I discovered when the new becomes comfortable, it's important to emerge beyond the limits of the new comfort zone. The breakthrough came when I realized that running a business always involves personal growth and transformation.

I was building relationships with my customers, but I forgot—crazy as it sounds—to entertain my relationship with my business. I never asked what it needed from *me*. It never crossed my mind to investigate what changes my business (and I) were going through, let alone to value and support it.

From then on, I started to focus on the transformation people *and* businesses undergo. I learned that engaging in conscious self-growth is crucial for business owners and "authorpreneurs." Running your own business changes who you are in profound ways. If you neglect how your personal growth is involved, your business can drag you down. This is why many authors get stuck and sabotage themselves. They're resisting their growth process or are ignorant of the internal transformation that writing a book always entails.

By the way, this doesn't only happen while writing. All creative activities bring about personal transformation (ultimately, our whole life is one big transformation, but that's a concept for another chapter).

What is an unusual habit you have as an entrepreneur and how does it help you persevere?

I have several.

In the morning, I envision completing the project I'll be working on that day with ease.

I always start with the finish line in mind. I observe how the thought of achieving the project makes me feel. I change everything that feels uncomfortable. Then I visualize successfully completing the project or task, which allows me to feel the satisfaction of finishing it. This process usually takes about five minutes.

When I experience how a finished project feels first, I see many more possibilities than when I just make a plan and start. Even if the plan is thorough, experiencing the feeling of accomplishment, really widens my perspective. It also trains my subconscious mind that accomplishing goals is a satisfying adventure.

I write my goals for the day on a piece of paper that has a motivational quote on it. Then I stick the paper on the wall in my office. Every time I finish a task, I strike it off the list and take a moment to feel how great it is that I've completed it.

Taking a moment to pause after completing a task allows me to have a small break before moving on to work on my next activity. That thing is done; no need to think about it anymore. Now I can start fresh on the next one.

This routine might sound silly, but it makes me stay focused and motivated. It is an antidote to the fear of failure and other negative emotions.

In the evening, I quickly go through what I accomplished that day and allow myself to feel good about it. If I was unable to achieve one of my goals, I forgive myself. In my mind, I change everything that didn't go well. It doesn't matter if it's possible or not. Then I let it go.

Further, I'm always trying to gain a deeper understanding of what's going on. What lies under the surface of what's happening? What is the real reason I did what I did? What is it that I'm doing right now in my life? I mean, *really* doing. Am I supporting my priorities, or am I buttering up my ego? Am I soothing my laziness with excuses that, deep down, I know are bullshit?

Asking myself these questions helps me get to know myself and keeps my motives pure. For example, I may think that I said yes to a request because I saw it as an opportunity. Yet, when I dug a little deeper, it turned out I was actually afraid of missing out on something.

I have an honest conversation with myself every day.

Another habit I have is to sort out my thoughts by writing them out by hand rather than using some tools on the computer. Something as small as writing down keywords for an ad and then drawing a frame around them is enough to get my creative juices flowing.

When you write things out by hand, you're using the right side of your brain, which is your creative hemisphere. From there, you tend to judge and analyze less. It can help you disconnect from any doubts, fears, or distractions. Your inner critic gets less of a chance to trash your activity, and you're more open to receiving creative ideas.

How have you used a book for your business?

Holding your own book in your hands is a magical experience. Apart from the fact that it makes you proud and polishes your self-confidence, it puts you ahead of the game and provides you with credibility. It's a great business card—at least if it's a high-quality book.

Having your own book is highly practical, too. I use my books as a way to spread my core message of how to build a strong inner foundation, step into your full power, and create on a higher level.

I love exploring the deeper truths behind things and uncovering new perspectives on life. When I discover a perspective that shifts my consciousness, I'm eager to share it with others. I'm as happy as a child when they tell me that their new outlook is working for them. What better way to share it than a book?

Besides spreading my message, I use my books as a way to give my mentees an introduction to my philosophy and method. When people read my book first, they are already clear about certain things. It enhances the quality, efficacy, and the value of my services.

This brings me to writing a book for your business.

Many business owners believe they aren't skilled or creative enough to write a book, but everybody has a book inside them, even if they can't write. In that case, you can hire a professional service to help you and do it anyway.

Writing a book is an excellent way to make a deeper connection with yourself. You will understand yourself and your motives better. This can improve your life and your business exponentially. Also, a book is many times better than a brochure or flyer. Books give your business a professional look. They also showcase the hidden talents inside you.

Most importantly, they remind you of who you are and what you stand for.

How do you make money from your books? How do you ensure this will continue to happen?

My first focus is on selling as many books as possible because I want to spread my message to as many people as possible—especially to those people who don't have enough resources to hire a coach or mentor.

After I created a book, I convert it into multiple products. I also produce trainings based on my books. Sometimes, I provide writing services.

To ensure my business is (and stays) profitable, it's important to keep up with new developments. I continually educate myself on new trends in the publishing world and marketing techniques. Further, I find it important to deepen the relationship with my partners and be surrounded by people who inspire me. Having a wise mentor is essential, too.

What bad advice do you often hear on the subject of authorship or writing a book for your business?

The advice worst advice I ever got was, "If you want to write a book, just do it."

Authors are creative, intuitive beings, and a book often "writes itself," but it's easy to get lost in the writing process. Your imagination takes you from here to there and from there to everywhere. It can be interesting to let your creative thoughts wander, as you may end up with a brilliant piece of text. However, it still probably needs to be put in a logical order (unless you're writing a surrealistic novel about chaos, of course).

Putting all your ideas together and making a coherent whole out of it is hard work. After all, you are trying to tie hundreds or thousands of sentences into a brilliant piece of art. Can you imagine having to put hundreds of pages together in a way that ultimately (you hope) astonishes the reader? I can tell you from personal experience, it's hell.

My mantra is: make a plan and a solid structure first, and only then "just do it."

When you write a nonfiction book (like I do), you should define at least the following points: What questions do you want to answer in your book, and in what order? And why do those questions matter?

Another bad bit of advice was the one I gave myself: "Do everything yourself. It's exciting. You learn new skills, and the creative process is a lot of fun." I'm telling you, don't fall into the same trap. Don't fool yourself. Writing and publishing is a very intensive process. Get as much support as you can afford. Don't be cheap on yourself when it comes to publishing your book.

It's essential to have a professional cover and a good editor. Cheap labor is, ultimately, expensive because oftentimes the work is not good enough and you have to do it again. But don't go into the business with somebody just because they are a famous expert, either. Your book represents who you are and what you stand for. The people who read and engage with your book must resonate with your vision and values. Therefore, you need to find the right balance between listening to your gut and trusting the advice of an experienced professional—even if your ego wants to have its own way.

If you lost everything—your book, your list, your products, your platform, your fame—and nobody knew who you were, what would you do in the next 30 days to get back on track, and what role would a book or publication take in the process?

First, I'd take a deep breath and allow myself to feel what I'm feeling. Then, I'd use my common sense to try and analyze the situation and make a plan.

If everything went down and we had no internet and, consequently, no way to access our email or social media, there would be widespread panic. However, I don't think I would panic that much. Even if I lost everything, I would still have my internal talents, skills, and know-how.

After all, I've experienced life without the internet, and I managed to build a successful business then. I know what tactics work in an internet-free world.

The only real challenge would be that I'd be limited to engaging with prospects in my area rather than working internationally like I do now.

In any case, I'd start with writing a (non-fiction) book and making a rock-solid plan that has a realistic timeframe for each phase. First, I would need to make sure I was clear about my true motives. I would ask myself a few questions, such as:

- Why do I want to start my activity? For example, to achieve financial freedom? To share my knowledge with the world? Or because I crave fulfilling work?
- If I can share that knowledge and obtain that freedom or satisfaction of a job well done, what will I be able to do then?
- If I can do that, what else is possible?

- If that is possible, what does it mean to me? How will I feel then?

Perhaps I will feel free and excited, or inspired to explore my creativity more. But I may also find I feel satisfied because I received recognition, which makes me feel better about myself. However, this is not the right kind of motivation, because it's based in fear that I'm not good enough. If I make a strategy based on a selfish, fear-driven motivation, my prospects will feel that, and will not trust me.

Then I'd write down and envision the following:

- What do I need to start my new business (amount of money, products, services, mindset)?
- What steps do I need to take to accomplish my goal?
- What is the intended message of my book or activity?

Then I'd make a timeline.

I'd really home in on the essentials and make everything as simple (yet, high-quality) as possible. I'd write my vision and my message down and put it on my desk to remind myself every day where I intend to go. My message is the advice I would give to my younger self, when she was in a situation where she couldn't see her next step. Therefore, my readers are people who encounter the same kind of challenges I've had then.

I'd also formulate a rough, long-term strategy to make sure my current vision has room to grow.

Then I'd start building connections with other authors and partners to become stronger together. Connections are like a multi-volume book. When carefully compiled, all the volumes add to the value of each part, and enhance the reader's experience.

I would always go for business partnerships where the parties involved complement each other and offer valuable services. Also, staying under one umbrella is attractive to clients because they do not have to search for products or services they need in other places. We could, for example, offer done-for-you services in multiple fields.

But if internet wasn't down and everything was operating correctly...

My plan would depend on whether I'd have some resources to spend on building my new business or if I have to start from scratch.

In the latter, my first priority would be to partner with a relatively famous author, blogger, or podcaster who writes on a topic that is similar to my own in order to build an email list of interested readers. To do that, I'd do the following:

1. I'd make sure I really understood what the author/blogger/podcaster is talking about, and ensure that I resonate with what they stand for.

2. Next, I'd create a small but high-quality ebook that complements one of the "celebrity's" books or activities. If possible, I'd hire a professional editor to review it to ensure that the material is not only good but is conveyed in an engaging way. I'd also create a simple but professional website, and three small products. On my website, I'd announce I'm working on a book (the one I mentioned above), and write a couple posts about it. I'd make an opt-in for people who are interested in knowing more about the topic.

Then I'd offer this ebook to the celebrity as a gift. In my ebook I'd include an opt-in page for another free product and a link to my website. This action should help me get some publicity and, hopefully, gather some email addresses.

If the author/blogger/podcaster is satisfied with my first product, I'd offer him or her another gift. This would be a complement to the first ebook I offered them.

3. Later on, I'd elaborate the ebook I offered to the celebrity and I'd put it on Amazon (or wherever it would be appropriate) as my business card. I'd promote it as best as I can, depending on my resources.

4. I'd create more simple additional products from my book. For example, workbooks, audiobooks, or small courses.

With that said, if I lost everything, and nobody knew who I was, and if I had the financial ability to do so, I'd reverse the process. I'd hire a reliable publishing service to help me edit and launch my first ebook (or another product) successfully. Then I'd choose a company who shares the same values as I do. I'd study them profoundly, and I'd write a small, appealing book about them and their services. I'd offer it to them and then propose to further develop the book so they could use it as an inspiring gift to their customers or employees.

I would even consider employing a marketing agency that resonates with my values to do the grunt work for me, so I could focus on creating products and building relationships with readers and potential partners as fast as possible. In the meantime, if I didn't know anything about the marketing, I'd make sure I'd educate myself on it. Knowledge is power, after all.

Laura can be reached at EssenSense.com

28

IT'S ABOUT THE AUDIENCE BY ERIC VAN DER HOPE

What is your business?

Book publishing and launch strategist.

What have been the key factors to your success and why?

That's a great question. There are many factors that can contribute to success in life and/or in business. Some of these factors changed based on the circumstances of my life and where I was at in my personal development as a person. The following are just some of the factors I credit to my success:

- Resiliency
- Empathy
- Conscientiousness
- Practicing receptiveness
- Maintaining a growth mindset

- Passion
- Supporting of teamwork

However, it's not sufficient enough to assume that practicing these qualities will guarantee success. I had to keep in mind that it wasn't about about me, it was about my audience—my tribe.

The main focus was making sure I knew the answers to the following:

- My audience's biggest problems
- What my audience's wants were
- What my audience's needs were
- What my audience was asking for

That's when you discover who your message is actually for. Focusing on that made me realize it's not about me—it's about my audience.

This helped me realize what my audience wanted. It wasn't just a message, but a message that impacts lives.

What is an unusual habit you have as an entrepreneur and how does it help you persevere?

That's a fascinating question. After giving it some thought, an unusual habit is not how I'd describe it...

What gets me excited is knowing that whatever message I'm trying to deliver is having some type of impact on the individual receiving it. That excitement increases exponentially when I know that the person I've impacted directly is now able to help their audience as a result of my original message.

This ignites a fire in my heart and soul. This is what drives me to continue doing what I do.

How have you used a book in your business?

Publishing a book opens up so many doors, especially for authors looking for additional ways to grow their businesses.

Many authors write a single book. If it's nonfiction, don't focus solely on selling copies. It's actually more effective to use the book as a marketing tool. This will get you more attention and result in other business sales opportunities.

The following is a list of ways that I've used books in my business (this list is certainly not exclusive):

1. Books help start conversations about you.

When people you trust tell you to use something because it works really well, you listen, right? A book becomes your "spokesperson" and helps people talk about you and your business. This can be one of the most effective marketing tools ever.

Think about it for a moment. You personally might be in a situation where someone you know in your area of expertise gets more attention than you, even though you know more than them. Why are they getting all the attention? They've got a book.

When you publish a book, you automatically become a subject matter expert. You've become an authority, and if leveraged effectively, you'll get the attention.

My books have appeared in bookstores and libraries, and they have been used as subject matter in university curriculums. This doesn't happen by chance; it happens by learning how to leverage your book and create demand.

2. Books help build awareness of your authority, credibility, and expertise.

A published author becomes the subject-matter expert.

A small percentage of people actually write and publish books, so a book sets you apart from your competition. This helps build awareness and credibility.

Credibility is everything in business. Before people will want to do business with you, they'll want to trust and believe in what you have to say. When someone reaches out to you asking for further information, what kind of an impression do you think you'll make if you can tell them, "Let me send you my best-selling book"?

3. Books attract potential clients.

Once you become an author, you become an authority. People look to you as an expert. This ultimately results in people reaching out and requesting to work with you so they can learn from you personally. This could be in the form of "Done With You" or "Done For You" services. After writing my books, I generated extra revenue streams by providing book-launch coaching, consulting, and more.

4. Books can help you pay less taxes from expenses and other write-offs.

This doesn't need much explanation. Publishing a book and selling it literally means you are in the business of selling. You have started your own legitimate business. You'll be able to write off business expenses—from training, to conferences, to utilities, and so on. I guarantee it, you'll end up paying less in taxes!

How do you make money from your books? How do you ensure this will continue to happen?

It is absolutely possible to make lots of money from a book! After publishing my first book, I was fortunate enough to sell thousands of copies. It was incredibly satisfying to watch the money keep coming in, month after month.

Unfortunately, most authors will never make much money from their books, because they don't approach it the right way.

When an author can sell books consistently, the money will flow. However, focusing on just book sales is not the most efficient way to rely on a steady flow of capital.

I'm not saying it's impossible to make money selling books alone, but it's far easier to make money from leveraging a book!

A couple of my books I published a decade ago sold thousands. Admittedly, they don't make much in sales now. I'm okay with that, because even though I'm not making sales directly, I'm making up for it indirectly by as much as 10, 20, 30, up to 100 times more.

The co-founder of Book in A Box, Tucker Max, has a simple explanation on how to approach the challenge of making lots of money from a book. First, the right question needs to be asked in order to get the best answer. He said that there is a right way and a wrong way of asking how to make money from books. (ref. 1)

The wrong way is: "*How do I sell a lot of books?*"

The right way is: "*How do I use my book as a tool to make money?*"

If you can learn how to leverage your book effectively, you'll discover that you will not need to put all your time and effort into selling individual copies of your book.

The following are some examples of leveraging a book and turning it into a lead or profit-making tool. If you'd like to learn more about each of these areas, you'll find an abundance of resources online. I'll share a few references and recommendations that will give you a place to start if you are interested in learning more (none of these references are affiliate links):

1. Create a lead magnet and landing page with a book.

Reader Magnets: Build Your Author Platform and Sell more Books on Kindle

My Book

How To Use Your Book As A Lead Magnet For Your Business

https://happyselfpublishing.com/how-to-use-your-book-as-a-lead-magnet-for-your-business/

Example of Rob Kosberg's free book lead magnet:

https://www.publishpromoteprofit.com/freebook/

Example of Chandler Bolt's free book lead magnet:

https://selfpublishingschool.clickfunnels.com/order-form

How To Use Your Book As A Lead Magnet

https://scribewriting.com/how-to-use-your-book-as-a-lead-magnet/

23 Compelling Lead Magnet Ideas to Attract More Subscribers

https://www.simplestartup.net/23-compelling-lead-magnet-ideas-examples/

15 Different Types of Lead Magnets You Can Use to Entice Subscribers [+ Examples]

https://fancythemes.com/lead-magnets/

. . .

2. Develop online programs from a book.

3 Steps to Create an Online Course From Your Book

https://self-publishingschool.com/3-steps-to-create-online-course-from-your-books/

How to Create and Sell an Online Course: The Ultimate Guide

https://www.smartpassiveincome.com/online-course-creation-guide/

Self-Publishing School's "Course Building for Authors" (not always open for enrollment).

https://selfpublishingschool.lpages.co/course-building-for-authors/

Other online course resources:

How to Create Your First Online Course, with Amy Porterfield

https://www.chrisducker.com/podcast/how-to-create-your-first-online-course/

Learn Amy Porterfield's Secrets on How to Create and Sell Courses Online

https://www.bizmavens.com/create-and-sell-courses-online/

How to make money with an awesome online course: The Complete Guide:

https://socialtriggers.com/online-courses-create-and-sell/

David Siteman Garland's: "Create Awesome Online Courses"

https://www.createawesomeonlinecourses.com/

Maria Coz's: "Launch Your Signature Course"

https://www.launchyoursignaturecourse.com/

Danny Iny's: "Course Builders Laboratory"

https://coursebuilderslaboratory.com/

Jeanine Blackwell's: "Create 6-Figure Courses Virtual Bootcamp"

https://create6figurecourses.com/

3. Use the book as a marketing tool.

How To Use Your Book As Your Most Powerful Marketing Tool

https://www.trevorcrane.com/how-to-use-your-book-as-your-most-powerful-marketing-tool/

The World's Best Marketing Tool: Writing a Book

https://www.entrepreneur.com/article/273885

A book just might be your best marketing tool ... ever!

http://www.kellermedia.com/best-marketing-tool-ever/

How A Self Published Book Can Be A Magical Marketing Tool

https://www.huffingtonpost.com.au/2016/01/21/books-marketing-business_n_8985046.html

4. Use a book as a foundation to host and create online summits.

All of us need mentors and teachers to guide us on our life journey.

I was honored to host one of the largest online book publishing summits a couple years back. I couldn't have done it without the thorough training from Navid Moazzez, the man behind Virtual Summit Mastery™.

If you are interested in hosting your own summit, there is no better person to learn from than Navid. Not only has he hosted his own wildly successful summits, his students have proven success as well.

I'd like to share with you an epic blog post that Navid has prepared for anybody interested in hosting their own virtual summit: "Virtual Summit: The Ultimate Step-by-Step Guide To Hosting A Wildly Successful Online Summit." On top of that, he is giving away even more bonus material: his proven "Cheat Sheet," where he shares the exact steps to run a Virtual Summit.

https://navidmoazzez.com/virtual-summit/

5. Paid mastermind groups or subscriptions.

How to Set Up and Sell a Paid Mastermind Group

https://www.sidehustlenation.com/paid-mastermind-groups/

How to Start a Mastermind Group for Impact and Income

https://paulzelizer.com/mastermind-group/

9 Things To Know Before You Start Your Own Mastermind

https://www.forbes.com/sites/sarahkathleenpeck/2018/07/17/9-things-to-know-before-you-start-your-own-mastermind/#540dd4a37da7

How to Create and Run a Mastermind Group

https://www.passionforbusiness.com/articles/mastermind-group.htm

Start your own paid Mastermind group with Mike Capuzzi

https://thesixfigurecoach.com/mastermind-group/

6. Paid workshops and group teaching

4 Tips to Make Workshops Your Business's Next Secret Weapon

https://convertkit.com/make-workshops

How to Design and Deliver Your Own Money Making Workshops & Retreats

https://www.changingcourse.com/design-deliver-money-making-workshops/

The Live Paid Virtual Workshop

https://www.yourfirst1k.co/digital-product-live-paid-workshop

Making Money in Paradise with Seminars and Workshops

https://myworkfromhomemoney.com/making-money-seminars-workshops/

7. Coaching services or consultations

How to quickly start a coaching program that makes $500 an hour

https://videofruit.com/blog/start-coaching-program/

Ultimate Guide to Creating Coaching Packages

https://www.evercoach.com/ultimate-guide-to-creating-coaching-packages

How to Design Your Own Signature Coaching Program

https://www.universalcoachingsystems.com/create-own-coaching-program/

How to Build Your First Premium Coaching Package

http://www.carolinsoldo.com/how-to-build-your-first-premium-coaching-package/

The 5 Key Steps to Starting a 6-Figure Coaching Business in 2018

https://www.earlytorise.com/start-coaching-business/

Create a Signature Coaching Program

https://latishastyles.com/create-signature-coaching-program-get-clients/

Create Your Online Coaching Program & Profit from your Passions Transforming Lives

https://coachtrainingworld.com/create-your-online-coaching-program/

How to Start an Expert Coaching Business

https://debbieallen.com/how-to-start-an-expert-coaching-business/

8. Paid speaking gigs.

How to Find Paid Speaking Opportunities in Any Industry

https://thespeakerlab.com/paid-speaking-opportunities/

Advance Your Reach - Stage To Scale Method (Pete Vargas)

https://advanceyourreach.com/

https://advanceyourreach.com/about-old/pete-vargas/

How To Find Paid Speaking Gigs And Get Booked Consistently

https://speakinglifestyle.com/finding-speaking-gigs/

How to Locate Speaking Engagements - Free and Paid

https://nonfictionauthorsassociation.com/how-to-locate-speaking-engagements-free-and-paid/

My good friend Mike Fritz (of Engage Now): an example of how to make speaking part of your business

https://engagenowint.com/

9. Live seminars or retreats

Retreat Planning 101: How to Host Your Own Retreat

https://christinekane.com/retreat-planning-101-how-to-host-your-own-retreat-2/

8 Tips for Running Wildly Successful In-Person Events

https://www.copyblogger.com/live-events/

Retreat Blueprint Program

https://www.wanderlustentrepreneur.com/retreat-blueprint-program-eg/

From Start to Finish: How to Plan a Retreat People will Love https://convertkit.com/how-to-plan-a-retreat

How to Plan an Event: The Complete Event Planning Guide

https://www.wildapricot.com/articles/how-to-plan-an-event

Your Seminar Planning Checklist: 16 Steps to Success

https://www.eventbrite.com/blog/seminar-planning-checklist-ds00/

10. Online webinars

How to Create a Webinar for Free

https://mariahcoz.com/blog/how-to-create-a-webinar-free

How to Create a Webinar from Scratch in 10 Simple Steps

https://www.convinceandconvert.com/digital-marketing/

How to Run a Webinar The Definitive Guide

https://webinarninja.com/how-to-run-a-webinar/

How to Do a Webinar Your Audience Will Love

https://www.wordstream.com/blog/ws/2014/08/26/how-to-do-a-webinar

I've just shared ten different income streams that could range anywhere from zero dollars (a lead magnet) to tens of thousands of dollars (paid masterminds).

What bad advice do you often hear on the subject of authorship or writing a book for your business?

I'd like to answer this question by sharing some of the mistakes that many authors make. Many of these mistakes could have resulted from bad advice from any number of sources.

1. Failing to develop a book-business marketing plan and launch plan.

2. Failing to build an audience prior to the book getting published.

3. Waiting to market the book until it's published (not pre-selling copies of the book).

4. Working without a book coach or publishing strategist, or taking advice from non-experts.

5. Not understanding your target market or audience.

6. Not having a basic understanding of ISBNs.

7. Trying to wear too many hats.

8. Getting too overwhelmed.

9. Not seeing the big picture from the start.

10. Publishing independently and naming the company after themselves.

11. Failing to understand what copyright is.

12. Not coming up with a good book title.

13. Trying to design your own book cover rather than hiring a professional.

14. Cutting corners on professional editing (not hiring a professional).

15. Failing to build your author platform early.

16. Putting too much thought into writing a perfect book.

17. Not developing relationships with influencers in your area of expertise.

18. Treating publishing like it's a hobby.

19. Thinking the book is meant for everybody.

20. Worrying about pleasing everybody.

21. Failing to get a proof sample before the book is published.

22. Not understanding the importance of email marketing and list building.

23. Deciding to only sell your book through one distributor.

24. Choosing to rush the publishing process.

25. Failing to optimize the book description.

26. Deciding not to have someone read your book before it gets published.

27. Failing to organize a proper book launch campaign.

28. Not reaching out to potential reviewers (for endorsements or advance reviews) ahead of time.

29. Failure to follow publishing submission guidelines.

That's just a sample list of the mistakes authors make. If you'd like a more thorough discussion on each of these topics and an explanation on how these mistakes can be fixed, grab my informative resource guide here: http://www.EricVanDerHope.com/resource-guide/

If you lost everything—your book, your list, your products, your platform, your fame—and nobody knew who you were, what would you do in the next 30 days to get back on track, and what role would a book or publication take in the process?

I'll start off sharing a simple foundation that begins with having an idea or topic you are already passionate about.

If you don't have an idea or something you are passionate about, do the following:

1 - Figure out what you're passionate about.

What lights you up, what burns in your soul!?

Sit down and brainstorm. Make a note of everything that comes to mind. When you come up with a list, choose the top five that really get you excited.

Now, of those five things, what can you see yourself doing every day? What would you love to be able to discuss, talk, write, or teach about every day? What would you never get tired of?

There is a good chance that one of those five things will stand out the most. Make that your choice.

2 - Research.

Once you've got your idea, topic, or message that your heart and soul is telling you to share, it's time to research it. Collect as much information, resources, blog posts, articles, and books that will contribute to learning more about what you chose.

. . .

3 - Start a newsletter/blog or create a community.

1. Create a newsletter or blog (this will help grow your email list).

2. Build a Facebook group.

By doing both, you will be building a community and a way to connect directly with your audience. By creating a group as well as a newsletter, the opportunity to engage with the people you connect with will increase. This will ensure you a solid foundation and help build your credibility, authority, and trust.

4 - Learn the mechanics of email marketing.

Learn the mechanics of building an email list, capturing subscribers, using an autoresponder or CRM service, and sending out email messages to your audience.

Here are some resources on how to build your list:

"List Building 101: How To Build an email List" (by Derek Halpern)

https://socialtriggers.com/list-building

"How to Build an Email List from Scratch: 10 Incredibly Effective Strategies" (by Hubspot)

https://blog.hubspot.com/marketing/list-building

"How To Build An Email List" (by Joanna Penn)

https://www.thecreativepenn.com/how-to-build-an-email-list/

"Want to go from 0 to 1,000 email subscribers in 30 days?" (by Bryan Harris)

https://videofruit.com/rapid-list-building/

"How to Use Social Media for Email List Building" (by Aaron Chichioco)

https://www.socialmediatoday.com/news/how-to-use-social-media-for-email-list-building/551142/

"A Step-by-Step Guide for Creating a Magnetic Email Incentive" (by Michael Hyatt)

https://michaelhyatt.com/email-incentive/

Here are some suggestions on the types of software available to automate your eMail communication:

· InfusionSoft

· Active Campaign

· ConvertKit

· Ontraport

· Aweber

· GetResponse

· Mailchimp

· Office AutoPilot

· Constant Contact

· Autoresponse Plus (ARP Reach)

· 1ShoppingCart

. . .

5 - Build a website.

Purchase your domain and host your website somewhere. There are many to choose from:

- Hostgator

- GoDaddy

- Bluehost

- 1&1

- iPage

- GreenGeeks

- FatCow

- A Small Orange

- Hostwinds

- DreamHost

- SiteGround

After picking your host, build your website by installing a Wordpress site. Most hosts have plug'n'play software that will help install a Wordpress site directly onto your domain.

6 - Learn how to create income from your newsletter/group.

I'll share two techniques, but there are literally hundreds:

a. Sell advertising.

b. Create a product.

You can offer to sell advertising space in your newsletter or blog. The larger your audience gets, the more you can charge for an advertising spot.

By engaging with your audience from within your community, you can learn very quickly what their pain points are and what they are having difficulties with. Develop a product that'll help solve your audience's problems.

7 - Continue to research additional topics and engage with your audience.

Prepare another newsletter or blog post with new material. Continue to engage with your audience, and you'll discover this can be repeated over and over again.

As a result of all the content you've created, this could be the beginning of an outline for many books to come!

It's important to understand the big picture here. You are building a solid foundation for creating relationships. All of us connect with other people, so by engaging with your audience and building credibility and authority, your audience will trust you and look to you for answers. They will want a closer connection to you and get it by purchasing whatever you have.

The following checklist is a more detailed action plan to facilitate your message:

1. Decide what you want to do.

2. Create your vision and goals.

3. Identify your market.

4. Create your business name.

5. Set up your business structure.

6. Make a business plan.

7. Obtain required permits or licenses.

8. Set up your home office.

9. Secure a domain name.

10. Create a pre-launch page and start building your website.

11. Choose a mail delivery service.

12. Create an email list or lead magnet.

13. Create an email auto-responder.

14. Create a series of sequential emails.

15. Develop your marketing plan.

16. Engage with your audience within groups or communities.

17. Reach out and engage with influencers.

18. Reach out as a guest to bloggers' podcasts.

19. Focus on a couple social media profiles.

20. Create a video for your product or service.

21. Create a landing page for you book or product.

22. Send press releases to media.

23. Sign up to the HARO report.

24. Consider paid advertisement.

25. Follow up with prospects.

26. Follow up with current customers.

27. Continually educate yourself through trainings, seminars, masterminds, and so on.

28. Build a press or media kit.

29. Set up a referral or affiliate program.

30. Dry-run your ordering process.

31. Launch your message or product.

What I've observed over the years is that many authors struggle the most with marketing--not just the physical part of the process, but also the mindset.

Marketing involves lots of effort and leg work on your part. You have to create a demand for your book. Give reason for your audience to purchase your book. Unfortunately, books aren't going to sell themselves.

There is no end to creating demand. It doesn't matter if you already launched or not. You create demand by simply growing your platform, marketing, advertising, promoting, and so on.

Tell your audience about the book. Reveal how it will impact and educate them. Focus on the problems and reveal how the book can fix or solve the problem. Create scarcity or tease your audience.

There is so much you can do to create a demand for your book. It's a 24/7 job. You have to reach out to influencers, collaborate, grow your audience, contact stores and libraries, utilize word of mouth. It requires a multitude of strategies.

Marketing a book means you have to start up to a year in advance and years more after.

Think of your book as a product. Just like any product, you must market it. Products aren't marketed once. You see advertisements on TV every day, right? Same for your book. You have to market it consistently over the long-term if you want the sales to continue.

Marketing is a marathon, not a sprint. You have to find time. There is no short-cut.

If you are searching for methods that if done correctly will be most effective, do a deep dive on Amazon Advertising Ads (also known as AMS ads). You have to invest in yourself if you want results.

Purchase some programs on how to use AMS effectively, or purchase some programs that teach you how to market books or build your author platform. There are a ton of programs online that provide this type of instruction. When you search and find articles, filter by date so you get the most recent info.

There are also a ton of Facebook groups that are specifically geared toward marketing. Do a search and you'll find some groups you can join for free.

There are literally hundreds of different marketing techniques that can be used to market books or products. What may have worked for me may not necessarily work for you, so you have to do the research, choose what you want to do, then do it. If it works, great. If it doesn't, move on to the next method.

Here are some inexpensive or no-cost ways to market your books (this stuff takes time and effort to do):

· Working and building your brand is extremely important to strengthening your credibility.

· Start with developing a website and or blog.

·   Use social media effectively (Facebook, Twitter, LinkedIn, YouTube).

·   Pre-marketing/promotion.

·   Organize a virtual (or physical) book tour.

·   Start guest blogging.

·   Be a guest on podcasts.

·   eZine marketing.

·   Article marketing.

·   Collaborate with folks in your genre/space.

·   Consider doing joint ventures.

·   The proper use of press releases.

The list goes on and on and on!

If you want to know how to use these methods, Google is your best friend.

There are many books on marketing in libraries and on the internet. Doing the proper research and learning how other successful authors do it will point you in the right direction.

Marketing is something that has to be done consistently, or your "message" gets lost in the "noise."

Here's an extensive list of great books that come to mind:

- *1001 Ways to Market Your Books*, by John Kremer
- *Platform: Get Noticed in a Noisy World*, by Michael Hyatt
- *Your First 1000 Copies: The Step-by-Step Guide to Marketing Your*

Book, by Tim Grahl

- *Jump Start Your Book Sales*, by Mariyln & Tom Ross
- *Plug Your Book*, by Steve Weber
- *Do It! Marketing: 77 Instant-Action Ideas to Boost Sales, Maximize Profits, and Crush Your Competition*, by David Newman
- *How To Publish and Promote Online*, by M.J. Rose & Angela Adair-Hoy
- *How To Make Real Money Selling Books*, by Brian Jud
- *5-Minute Book Marketing for Authors: Easy and effective ways to market your book every single day!*, by Penny C. Sansevieri
- *Publicize Your Book*, by Jacqueline Deval
- *The Right Way To Write, Publish and Sell Your Book*, by Patricia L. Fry
- *Bestselling Book Publicity*, by Rick Frishman & Robyn Freedman Spizman
- *Facebook Marketing an Hour a Day*, by Chris Treadaway & Mari Smith
- *Twitter Revolution*, by Deborah Micek & Warren Whitlock
- *The New Rules of Marketing & PR*, by David Meerman Scott
- *Guerrilla Social Media Marketing*, by Jay Conrad Levinson & Shane Gibson
- *The Author's Guide to Marketing Books on Amazon*, by Rob Eagar
- *Guerrilla Marketing for Writers*, by Jay Conrad Levinson, Rick Frishman, Michael Larsen & David L. Hancock
- *Publish. Promote. Profit: The New Rules of Writing, Marketing & Making Money with a Book*, by Rob Kosberg
- *Book Marketing DeMystified*, by Bruce Batchelor
- *Social Media*, by Chris Brogan
- *Authorpreneur: Build the Brand, Business, and Lifestyle You Deserve*, by Jesse Warren Tevelow
- *Book Marketing Made Easy*, by D'vorah Lansky
- *The Frugal Book Promoter*, by Carolyn Howard-Johnson

- *Red Hot Internet Publicity*, by Penny C. Sansevieri
- *Launch to Market: Easy Marketing For Authors*, by Chris Fox
- *Influencer: Building Your Personal Brand in the Age of Social Media*, by Brittany Hennessy
- *Mastering Amazon Ads: An Author's Guide*, by Brian D. Meeks
- *One Million Followers: How I Built a Massive Social Following in 30 Days*, by Brendan Brendan
- *The Influential Author: How and Why to Write, Publish, and Sell Nonfiction Books that Matter*, by Gregory V. Diehl
- *Gap Selling: Getting the Customer to Yes: How Problem-Centric Selling Increases Sales by Changing Everything You Know About Relationships, Overcoming Objections, Closing and Price*, by Keenan
- *How to Market a Book (Third Edition)*, by Joanna Penn
- *Publishing 101: A First-Time Author's Guide to Getting Published, Marketing and Promoting Your Book, and Building a Successful Career*, by Jane Friedman
- *The Holy Grail of Book Launching*, by Mimi Emmanuel
- *Guerrilla Publishing: Revolutionary Book Marketing Strategies*, by Derek Murphy
- *Ultimate Guide to Platform Building*, by Wendy Keller
- *World Wide Rave: Creating Triggers that Get Millions of People to Spread Your Ideas and Share Your Stories*, by David Meerman Scott
- *The Write Way: Everything You Need to Know About Publishing, Selling and Marketing Your Book*, by Amy Collins
- *The Ultimate Guide to Writing and Marketing a Bestselling Book - on a Shoestring Budget*, by Dee Blick
- *Build Your Author Platform: The New Rules: A Literary Agent's Guide to Growing Your Audience in 14 Steps*, by Carole Jelen and Michael McCallister
- *Create Your Writer Platform: The Key to Building an Audience,*

Selling More Books, and Finding Success as an Author, by Chuck Sambuchino

- *The Extroverted Writer: An Author's Guide to Marketing and Building a Platform*, by Amanda Luedeke
- *Engagement from Scratch!: How Super-Community Builders Create a Loyal Audience and How You Can Do the Same!*, by Danny Iny
- *The Nonfiction Book Marketing Plan: Online and Offline Promotion Strategies to Build Your Audience and Sell More Books*, by Stephanie Chandler
- *This Is Marketing: You Can't Be Seen Until You Learn to See*, by Seth Godin
- *All Marketers are Liars: The Underground Classic That Explains How Marketing Really Works--and Why Authenticity Is the Best Marketing of All*, by Seth Godin
- *Indie Author Book Marketing Success: Proven 5-Star Marketing Techniques from Successful Authors and Book Marketing Experts*, by Shelley Hitz, et al.
- *Reader Magnets: Build Your Author Platform and Sell more Books on Kindle*, by Nick Stephenson
- *Marketing Your Book On Amazon: 21 Things You Can Easily Do For Free To Get More Exposure and Sales*, by Shelley Hitz
- *The Nonfiction Book Marketing Plan: Online and Offline Promotion Strategies to Build Your Audience and Sell More Books*, by Stephanie Chandler
- *Book Marketing is Dead: Book Promotion Secrets You MUST Know BEFORE You Publish Your Book*, by Derek Murphy

That's just a handful of books, there is plenty of information that can be found online or offline (in libraries) to figure out the how and what.

This is just the tip of the iceberg!

Check out Chandler Bolt's epic article, "Book Marketing: Best Practices for Higher Sustained Book Sales."

https://self-publishingschool.com/book-marketing-how-to-skyrocket-sales-of-your-book/

I'd recommend creating a marketing plan. Lay out the steps to achieve your goals, then follow the plan. Otherwise, you'll be totally overwhelmed.

Every person has the ability to create their own unique marketing plan. There are a ton of resources at the tip of your fingers. If you simply search, "book marketing plan" on Google or Amazon, you'll discover many, many, *many* versions of book marketing plans and templates.

A good place to start would be to check out some of my favorite book marketing templates, created by some reputable friends of mine:

Tim Grahl's checklist:

https://booklaunch.com/book-marketing-checklist/

Nick Thacker's book marketing plan:

http://www.writehacked.com/self-published-book-marketing-plan/

Jennifer Mattern's "Book Marketing Timeline: From Pre-launch to Post-launch:"

https://allfreelancewriting.com/book-marketing-timeline-from-pre-launch-to-post-launch/

Want to learn how to write a book marketing plan? Here is a simple checklist on getting started:

https://www.standoutbooks.com/13-steps-to-write-a-book-marketing-plan/

. . .

Let's revisit the principle ideas that should be foremost in your mind to help you refocus and redefine your idea, product, or message.

-- Develop your business plan.

To be successful in business you must be professional in your business approach, which means before you do anything else--before you think of a name, before you develop a product, before you even take the first step to follow through on a niche market idea--you must first establish a business plan.

You will not get anywhere if you do not know where you are going.

A business plan ultimately consists of three distinct parts. The initial part outlines all the key elements of the business you intend to develop. It makes initial financial projections, indicates the intended structure, lists personnel to be recruited for the company, and other sundry details.

The next section is the marketing plan. This outlines the steps you intend to take to reach your target audience. First, define your target audience and describe your ideal customer. Then draw up a preliminary budget for advertising and indicate how your efforts will be monitored and refined over time.

The third section of your plan outlines the underlying strategy of your company. Your strategic plan should outline the values of your company and how you will incorporate those values into your business model.

-- Setting realistic milestones and goals.

Goal setting is an essential element to success. It applies as readily to success in a person's personal life as it does to business. There are, however, a few key points about goal setting that most people miss.

The most important note about goal setting is that you must be realistic in the milestones you create, whether they are for your business or for you personally. Challenge yourself by all means, but don't set the bar so high that you can't possibly overtake it. Done correctly, goal setting should enhance your confidence in yourself and your ideas. It should help you see the positive as well as the negative elements of your business, improving both in turn.

-- You must have the desire to achieve the goals.

Another essential ingredient to business success is the desire to achieve. There's absolutely no point in going into business for yourself unless this is something that you really want to do. You must have a passion for it and understand *why* you are doing what you are doing.

If you don't *really* want to achieve your goals, you're not going to enjoy the road to success.

-- You must mentally visualize the possibilities.

If you have a plan, you've set your goals, and you know you really want to publish your book, create your product, or share your message, you most likely have the right mental vision and focus. The more time you spend planning, the clearer the process will look. The more clear and focused your vision, the more likely you are to take the appropriate action to achieve success in your market.

-- You must be able to take action to produce your desired results.

The final point I'd like to emphasize is that you must follow through on your plans to be successful. Taking action does not simply mean getting a website and writing a book on a chosen subject. It is a far broader notion than this, and yet also far more specific. To be successful, you must calculate your approach. You must plan. When you act, your actions must be calculated to achieve a desired effect. You must be conscious of the actions you take with from day one. You must follow through on your plans, but you must also be prepared to extend yourself, constantly testing and refining your business to maintain the most important component of business success: the good will of your potential customers.

Keep your goals in mind, but above all: have fun doing it!

Eric can be reached at ericvanderhope.com.

29

BE UNSTOPPABLE BY QAT WANDERS

What is your business?

Wandering Words Media: an editing and ghostwriting ("spiritwriting") company specifically built to provide traditional-publishing-quality editing in the self-publishing world. I also have the Wandering Wordsmith Academy, where I train authors to become editors (thereby saving thousands and thousands of dollars on editing over time!).

What have been the key factors to your success and why?

Mentors. Hands down. I have invested *so* much in one-on-one mentoring, online courses, coaching, conferences, seminars, and training. I am never without a paid mentor (or two or three). I wouldn't be where I am if I had been too scared to invest in these things. Putting myself into debt over it was the best thing I ever did.

What is an unusual habit you have as an entrepreneur, and how does it help you persevere?

Working with *zero* deadlines. I don't do them. Not anymore. Just . . . no. I tried at the beginning but ended up burned out and overwhelmed (plus a minor stroke and heart attack in my 30s). So I work when I feel like it. It allows me to enjoy myself more, which, in turn, means I work efficiently.

Efficiency is key in my life. I'm a single mom, and I literally built a business empire from scratch in just a few years.

I went from living in a van as a traveling circus performer for over a decade—and no, I'm not kidding—to settling down, fighting for custody of my daughter, and building a company completely by myself. I did this with zero support system. It was just me. Desperately trying to figure out how to build and run a business while getting my little girl to band practice, swim lessons, and Girl Scout meetings.

My health started to go downhill quickly, and I worked myself into the ground. I thought I had to please everyone. I took every job I could get because I was desperate and didn't want to say no. I tried to adhere to everyone's deadlines and expectations.

I found myself neglecting my daughter after fighting so hard to keep her in my life. I was ignoring my health and all the warning signs that this had become too much for me.

It took a full-blown nervous breakdown for me to finally realize I couldn't please everyone, and it was pointless to even try. The universe will look out for us if we have faith. I honestly believe that.

With that in mind, everything started to shift for me. I stopped agreeing to deadlines, and I started outsourcing the jobs I didn't enjoy or that took up too much of my time. Slowly, my schedule opened back up, and I was able to regain my sanity.

No matter what, I take time to go to yoga every day and also to spend quality time with my beautiful and intelligent little girl.

I learned I needed to say no to others so I could say yes to myself. As cliché as that may sound, it was quite the eye-opening epiphany for me when I was so career-oriented and high strung.

How have you used a book for your business?

It was an accident. I just wanted to get it out there quickly to please my dad. He was dying of cancer, and his dying wish was to see me become a best-selling author and hold my book in his hands. Leave it to my dad to expect me to move mountains! But it always worked, I guess, because it lit a fire under my butt for sure.

So I wrote what I thought I could crank out the fastest and knew the most about (aside from language), and that was yoga.

The book did insanely well. Aside from thousands in royalties the first month, it generated over $30,000 in income from leads in the first 30 days. So I wrote another . . . and it did even better.

I used the success of my yoga books as fodder for my editing and spiritwriting business. The credibility proved I knew what I was doing.

How do you make money from your books? How do you ensure this will continue to happen?

I made $42,000 in royalties last year (2018). And that was just from Amazon. That came from five books with very little marketing. But it's nothing compared to my spiritwriting and editing income. Since I published my first book, I built my business from zero to six figures in less than six months, and I've doubled my profit margin each quarter since.

But what excites me most is what I am working on now. I have produced more than fifty rough drafts for YA urban fantasy novels over the past year and a half. I've published a handful of them already —including my latest series, *The Owl Shifter Chronicles*—and the rest are finally with my editing team. I'm getting covers made, and I have been studying ads and marketing into the wee hours of the night. I devised several launch strategies to test out, and I am raring to go!

On top of this, I have been helping my 10-year-old daughter (Ora Wanders) write and publish her own fantasy series. Her first book was a huge success; it won several awards and brought in enough royalties to pay for her trip to The Wizarding World of Harry Potter in Florida. We are even co-authoring a new series together as well.

I will continue with my non-fiction spiritual books, and I am even planning to release a few writing and editing books, but my 2019 focus is finally getting my fiction going (under Qatarina Wanders, not just Qat Wanders, to avoid confusion).

Plus, I have been building quite the platform, and I have helped hundreds of others produce successful books, so now it's my turn.

What bad advice do you often hear on the subject of authorship or writing a book for your business?

"Get everyone you know to buy and review your book on Amazon."

There are so many things wrong with that. One, Amazon will flag you for it if they notice, or even suspend your account (I know from experience).

Second, it totally screws with the algorithms and your "also boughts." It takes months for the bots to figure out who to show your book to after that.

Plus, it's just awkward. What if your friends and family don't want your book, or worse—what if they hate it? Then there is the five-star review dilemma. How awkward is it when your childhood buddy gives you three stars and claims your "character development needs work"? I can answer that: VERY!

If you lost everything—your book, your list, your products, your platform, your fame—and nobody knew who you were, what would you do in the next 30 days to get back on track, and what role would a book or publication take in the process?

I want my answer to be: "I would just put my nose down and get right back to writing my novels!" But, in reality, after probably having another nervous breakdown or stroke, I would start hustling for editing and ghostwriting work. It's good money, fast money, and I'm damn good at it. One good ghostwriting client, or a couple good editing clients, and I've made enough money to sustain me for a year.

And during that 30 days, I would start reaching out to other authors who want to learn how to edit. Training editors is a great passion for me because it allows me to help people save a ton of money on editing.

And just a disclaimer: I would never advocate editing your own book *entirely*. Even editors need editors. I hire a whole editing team for each of my books. But when you can do the majority of the editing on your own books, your editing costs are a fraction of the price they would be otherwise. To add to that, some people I've trained have gone on to turn editing into a career as well. So it's a win-win for everyone.

Maybe I've put a little too much thought into this whole 30-days question, but while I'm working on those projects, and training other editors, I would then use those editors to help me get my own books ready for publication. So, shortly after the 30 days are up, I would be ready to launch some of my own books once again.

I guess I would basically just redo everything I did to achieve all my success, but I would do it faster because now I know what I'm doing!

You can reach Qat at wanderingwordsmedia.com

30

BOOK TO BOSS FRAMEWORK BY SONYA AND PRIYA WADHERA

What is your business?

Our company, Book To Boss, helps authors leverage their books to become their own bosses. With our backgrounds as both authors and entrepreneurs, we founded the company because we saw a need to help authors sell more books and earn a full-time living from their writing. We believe the term, "starving artist," no longer has to be a reality.

Look at some of the most iconic and famous brands today, such as Harry Potter, Twilight, and Jurassic Park, and some of the most well-known experts, such as Tim Ferriss and Jack Canfield. They have all grown into multi-million-dollar businesses and continue to entertain and serve millions of people around the world. Yet, they all started with a single book.

How did they achieve this monumental success? By adopting a business mindset and turning their books into businesses with multiple products and services. That's exactly why we founded Book To Boss.

Through strategy sessions, coaching calls, and signature courses, we help authors build businesses around their books by creating complementary products and services. These serve as additional income streams they can use to provide more value to their customers all while growing their incomes. Ultimately, this allows authors to profit from their passions and live the lives they have always wanted. Using the Book To Boss method, we've seen authors go from making a few book sales to building a full-fledged business and brand.

What have been the key factors to your success and why?

There are a few factors that have helped us get to where we are today. The first factor has been to adopt a long-term mindset. By doing so, we have been able to create a grander vision for our business and build a solid foundation for the future. The awareness that we will be working on a business for a number of years has created new and exciting possibilities that wouldn't have been possible if we had simply launched a stand-alone project.

The second factor has been to always provide our customers with tremendous value. Whether it was a book we wrote or a client we coached, we always tried to ensure that we make a positive difference in our customers' lives. The famous quote by Robert Baden-Powell summarizes it best: "Try and leave this world a little better than you found it." We have implemented this philosophy by providing customers with the tools they need to be successful. This has created a positive cycle where customers have become our advocates and helped share our message with others. Providing value for our customers has become a key driving force behind our creativity and continued passion for our work.

Finally, we always remember to have fun! We find that creative inspiration strikes in our most joyful moments. This translates positively to our final products and makes for happier customers. It's a win-win!

What is an unusual habit you have as an entrepreneur, and how does it help you persevere?

We start our mornings by listening to a playlist of uplifting and motivational songs. These songs help put us in the right frame of mind for success and inspire us to start each day with excitement. The world of business is always changing, which makes entrepreneurship difficult and frustrating at times. It can be discouraging when we can't find an immediate solution to a problem we are facing. To avoid remaining in a negative mindset, our playlist of motivational music helps us shift into a more positive state and persevere through difficult problems.

How have you used a book for your business?

We have used our book to build a business in two ways. When we started, we created and sold multiple products that related to our book to complement the story and message. We used our book as a launching pad to build a larger brand and business with multiple income streams.

The second business, Book To Boss, came about as a happy accident! At various book signings across the country, fans would ask us about how they could create books of their own. They wanted advice on how they could share their unique stories with the world and build a brand around them, just as we had done. After the ninth or tenth time of getting this question, we knew we had a golden opportunity on our hands, and that's how Book To Boss was born! Now, in addition to selling our own branded products, we use our knowledge and experience to help others. Through our company, we help our clients create complementary products and services based on their books to help them build successful businesses of their own.

How do you make money from your books? How do you ensure this will continue to happen?

We make money from our books through multiple diversified streams of income. From the beginning, our vision was to build a business and brand around our book with multiple product offerings to keep our target market engaged and excited. In today's world, content is king, and customers consume content very quickly. If you don't have the next book or product planned, the customer will most likely move on to something newer and seemingly more exciting.

The most common question that our fans asked us was, "What's next?" Answering this question was the foundation from which we were able to continuously make money. Having our own complementary products, such as additional books, clothing, and merchandise, has allowed us to make significantly more than we would have if we just had a single book to offer. By increasing our product offerings, we were able to keep our fans engaged, which led to an increase in sales and kept them coming back.

This is the same "Book To Boss" framework we teach our clients. Before even writing a single word, we encourage them to create a grander vision for their books so they can branch out, create complementary products and services, and earn full-time incomes from their writing.

What bad advice do you often hear on the subject of authorship or writing a book for your business?

The one piece of bad advice that stands out to us can be summarized by the old adage: "Build it and they will come." With the fierce competition in today's society, there are so many products and services that customers have to choose from that it becomes difficult to stand out.

Using a "Build it and they will come" mindset can set an author up for failure. This is because it becomes infinitely harder for authors to make sales when they only start to think about marketing their books after they have been written.

Coming from a business background, we learned early on about the importance of identifying and understanding one's target market in order to build a strong platform to launch from. As we wrote our first book, we tailored elements of the message and story so that it would resonate with our target audience. Our goal was to create multiple products that our audience would actually want and find valuable. This made the process of writing and marketing our book much easier.

If you lost everything—your book, your list, your products, your platform, your fame—and nobody knew who you were, what would you do in the next 30 days to get back on track, and what role would a book or publication take in the process?

Although we've lost our book, list, products, and platform, we still have our knowledge and business expertise, so we know we will be able to create something amazing. We believe that everything is possible with confidence, commitment, a plan, and by taking massive action. The next 30 days will be overwhelming, but at the same time we find it exciting to build something new from scratch. It also helps that there are two of us because we can support each other, keep each other accountable, and split up tasks to get them done faster.

It will be a busy month, so we will spend most of our time and energy on the business. This means minimizing distractions like Netflix, having our favorite take-out place on speed dial, and creating a routine that allows us to focus the majority of our time on business tasks. We will also make sure to work out regularly and take a couple days off to relax and spend time with family and friends.

To get started, we will use the same advice we give to our coaching clients and implement our signature Book To Boss framework. Our goal is to use a book as the foundation to build a larger brand and business. Over the next 30 days, our focus will be to build a loyal fan base of people who can benefit from the book and products we offer. Below, we have outlined steps we will take to launch our business from scratch.

WEEK 1: THE GAME PLAN

This week will be about planning and setting up our business, so there will be a lot to do!

RESEARCH

Our first task will be to brainstorm the type of book we will write and select the niche it will be in. We will choose a niche that we are passionate about, knowledgeable in, and can add value to. Given the time constraint and our previous experience as children's book authors, we will write a children's book. The next step is all about understanding our target market. We will need to identify who they are, what they want, and where they hang out online. Our goal will be to determine what our target market values in order to create complementary products based on our book that we can sell in our business.

BOOK OUTLINE

Using our preliminary target market research, we will create an outline for our story and ensure that we tailor the message to something our target audience will resonate with. We will make sure our story and characters are unique and relevant so that they stand out and bring something new and exciting to the market.

BRANDING AND ILLUSTRATION DESIGN

At this point, the book outline will be detailed enough so that we can design the illustrations. We will focus on branding and pick an eye-catching color scheme and illustration style to use across our book and products. The fun part is always designing our characters and bringing them to life with their own unique personalities! We will also finalize our book title and business name so that we can create a design for the front and back cover of our book. Due to the tight deadline, we will keep the illustrations simple and ensure that the designs are completed by the end of the week so they are ready to send to an illustrator.

SOCIAL MEDIA PROFILE SET-UP

It's time to set up our social media profiles and pages. We will make sure all our profiles follow the same branding style; something that is fun and playful for kids. We will focus primarily on Facebook as a key platform to get traffic from, in addition to other marketing strategies as well.

PRODUCT SELECTION

We will finalize the list of additional products to offer alongside the book. These products will be something our target market would find valuable and be willing to pay for. We have decided to sell T-shirts and tote bags that feature the characters from our children's book. We have found that including merchandise in addition to the book helps kids feel more connected to the story and characters and builds stronger brand recognition. For launch day, we will be creating a special introductory offer with all the products bundled together at a discounted rate.

PRODUCT SOURCING, FULFILLMENT, AND DISTRIBUTION

Now that we have decided to sell books, T-shirts, and tote bags, we will do a thorough analysis of the associated product, packaging, fulfillment, and distribution costs. We will request quotes from different suppliers and order sample products to ensure our products are high quality and cost effective. We will select suppliers that offer turnkey solutions, including product creation, packaging, and fulfillment, so that we can focus on our core competencies. We will also determine a price for our products that ensures profitability and is in line with other competitors' products in the market. In a perfect world, by the end of the week, we will have determined the suppliers we will be using to fulfill our orders.

INFLUENCER MARKETING RESEARCH

Influencers have the ability to reach thousands of customers through their own networks. We will leverage this by creating a targeted list of potential influencers to reach out to in the coming weeks for partnerships. We will make sure that the message of our book aligns with the influencer's work and that we can provide great value to their audience.

WEEK 2: GETTING DOWN TO BUSINESS

ILLUSTRATIONS

We will hire an illustrator to complete the illustrations for each page of the book in addition to the front and back covers. Our goal will be to have the completed illustrations by the end of the week. We will ensure that at least one or two illustrations are completed earlier so that we can add them to our marketing materials and post some of them on social media.

WRITE THE BOOK

Using the outline we created, it's time to write the book. We will refer back to our target-market research and product offerings to ensure the message and story align. By the end of the week, we will have a completed version to send to an editor for review.

LEAD MAGNET CREATION

We will create a lead magnet that we can give away to our target audience in exchange for their email. We have decided to offer a free digital activity book with coloring pages and games because it is something entertaining for kids and helpful for parents. We will incorporate any completed illustrations in the activity book so that kids can start to familiarize themselves with the characters in our story.

WEBSITE AND LANDING PAGE CREATION

It's time to build our website and landing pages. We will make sure the platform we choose includes e-commerce functionality. For now, we just need the basics, but we will add all the bells and whistles to the site next week. We will install a Facebook pixel so we can begin to understand visitor behavior. We will also create a landing page on our website where we can advertise our free digital activity book. As marketers, we know that the page needs a captivating hook, engaging copy, and a clear call to action, so we will make sure our page has those elements. We will also create a thank you page that includes prominent social share buttons so visitors can share the digital activity book with their friends.

EMAIL SEQUENCES

We will write our email sequences and plan them into an autoresponder so that they are ready to go. We will focus on creating both a welcome email sequence and post-purchase email sequence that customers can automatically be added to. Our welcome sequence will be for people that download our digital activity book. The emails in this sequence will include an invitation to join a VIP club. The VIP club will give members early access to products, discounts, special perks, and bonuses, too. In the post-purchase follow-up sequence, we will ask for customer reviews and feedback so that we can use them as social proof on our website and social media profiles in the future. Lastly, we will ensure that we write any additional email broadcasts or sequences needed to promote our products during launch week.

SOCIAL MEDIA MARKETING

Marketing is one of the most important aspects of a business. You can have the best product in the world, but it won't matter if no one knows about it. So, we believe that it is important to have multiple strategies to connect with our target audience online.

We will begin by promoting the free digital activity book to our target audience by posting a link to the landing page on our social media profiles. This will help us build an initial email list of potential customers. We will also create and post entertaining content on social media for our audience to engage with. This will include daily Facebook live videos that feature information about our upcoming book and products as well as a behind-the-scenes look at our business. We will also run Facebook ads to help grow our audience. During the week, we will monitor our ads to make sure that they are optimized and effective. We will also join Facebook groups in our niche and start engaging with group members by answering questions to provide value. We will share our free digital activity book with group members that show interest in it so that we can continue building our list for launch day.

INFLUENCER OUTREACH

We will reach out to the list of influencers we found in week one to find out how we can partner with them. We will explain the benefits of working together and emphasize how we can add value to their audience through our high-quality product offerings. By the end of the week, we should hear back from some of them so we can schedule promotions for our launch week.

LAUNCH TEAM

We will start a launch team in order to help promote our book. To find members, we will ask people that are currently on our email list and also make a list of anyone we feel may be interested in joining the team.

WEEK 3: GOING THE DISTANCE

EDITING THE BOOK

We will send an editor a copy of our book for review. Although it's aggressive, our goal is to have the editing completed by the middle of the week. We feel this should be possible due to the fact that children's books have minimal text.

BONUS OFFER CREATION

Our goal is to connect with our customers and build a relationship with them over the long term. Since some customers may not purchase directly through our website, but instead through other retail platforms such as Amazon or Barnes & Noble, we will need a method for obtaining their contact information. To do this, we will create a bonus that customers can download as a thank you for purchasing our book. We will also create a bonus page on our website that customers can visit after they have purchased the book. This page will have a field to capture emails so that we have a way of contacting them post-purchase. We will include a link to the bonus page in the front of the book.

BOOK DESIGN

Once we have the edited book and illustrations in hand, we will have everything we need to put the book together! We will send the final text and illustrations to a book designer so that they can create the print- and ebook-ready files.

PRINT BOOK DISTRIBUTION

Once we have the print-ready files, we will send them to our supplier and complete a test order to make sure everything is ready for launch day. Since it is so close to launch day, we will have to overnight it to ensure we receive the print copy in time.

EBOOK DISTRIBUTION AND MARKETING

For the ebook version, we will distribute it globally on platforms such as Amazon, Barnes & Noble, Kobo, iBooks, and more. These platforms already have large amounts of traffic, so we will use them to increase our reach and potential customer base. To generate buzz and encourage people to purchase the book, we will run ads on Amazon and list our book on promotion sites.

PRODUCT AND ORDER TESTING

Once we receive the completed illustrations, we will select one illustration to feature on our T-shirts and tote bags. We will send the illustration files over to our suppliers so that they can add them to the products and packaging. As we chose suppliers that also do fulfill-ment, we will place a test order for each of our products to ensure the product quality, design, and packaging are exactly what we envi-sioned. We will also have to overnight the products due to the time crunch.

PRODUCT MOCKUPS

Since we know what our products will look like, we will have a graphic designer create 3D mockups that we can add to our website. This will really start to bring our products to life!

WEBSITE AND STORE UPDATES

With our illustrations and product mockups complete, we will update our website and create the following products in our store:

Product 1: Book

Product 2: T-shirts

Product 3: Tote bags

Product 4: Bundle: Print book, T-shirt, and tote bag

For launch week, we will create a special sales page that offers the product bundle at a discounted price. The offer will be time sensitive to encourage customers to take action. We will also test our full website and ordering system to ensure everything is working properly.

SOCIAL MEDIA MARKETING

This week, we will make sure that we stay consistent on social media by doing daily Facebook lives and engaging with members in Face-book groups. We will continue to run ads and promote our free digital activity book so that we can grow our email list.

BOOK TRAILER

We will also create short book trailers to promote our upcoming children's book. We have found this to be an effective marketing strategy because it helps get kids excited about the characters in the story. Once the book trailers are complete, we will upload them to YouTube. To promote the book trailers, we will send an email to our list and add the trailers to our social media profiles and our Goodreads and Amazon author pages.

LAUNCH TEAM

We will send copies of the finished ebook to our launch team once it is ready. In exchange for a free early review copy of the book, we will ask our launch team to share the book on their own blogs, social media platforms, and request that they leave an unbiased review on Amazon. We will include promotional materials that we have created, such as banners and scripts, to make it easier for them to share with their community.

INFLUENCER OUTREACH

Following up with influencers is important so that we can finalize any last-minute details for launch week. We will provide the influencers with a finished copy of the ebook and the artwork and copy they need to carry out the promotional campaign. We will also answer any questions they have to ensure that everything runs smoothly.

WEEK 4: IT'S SHOWTIME!

It's finally time to launch! This week, we will focus our efforts on marketing, outreach, and sales!

EMAIL MARKETING

We will send out multiple emails to the email list we have been building over the past few weeks. We will also ask our audience and

VIP club members to share the product bundle offer with their family and friends to help get the word out.

SOCIAL MEDIA PROMOTIONS AND INFLUENCER MARKETING

We will want to build on our current momentum, so we will continue to promote our offer on our social media profiles, run ads on Facebook and Amazon, and ensure that the influencer marketing campaigns are converting. We will track the performance of each of our marketing campaigns and tweak anything that isn't performing well.

LAUNCH TEAM

We will follow up with our launch team to check in and thank them for the work they have been doing to share and promote the book. We will also let them know about the special discounted bundle that we have available for launch week.

CELEBRATE AND PLAN FOR THE FUTURE!

It's time to celebrate all of the hard work and effort that we've put in over the past 30 days. It will be nice to receive initial feedback from new customers as we start to make sales. Our goal is for our book and products to be useful and bring our customers joy! Toward the end of the week, we will assess how things are going and continue to make any improvements necessary. We will also make sure to record all the lessons learned up until this point.

MOVING FORWARD...

We will continue to create and launch new books and products. To determine which products to sell next, we will do a survey of our current audience to see what they want. We will continue to stay consistent with our social media promotions and also explore new marketing opportunities, such as affiliate promotions and in-person events at schools, libraries, and bookstores, etc.

FINAL THOUGHTS...

We wish you the best of luck with setting up your own business. If you follow this process or even pieces of it, you will have huge success!

You can reach Sonya and Priya at booktoboss.com.

31

HIJACK THE TOPIC BY KENNY YAP

What is your business?

Life transformation using the art of Chinese metaphysics (Feng Shui, Chinese Astrology, etc.).

What have been the key factors to your success and why?

Failing faster than anyone else. No one can tell you if a strategy or tactic works except for the market itself. Testing is crucial, and you must be ever ready to kill your own ideas, never falling in love with them.

What is an unusual habit you have as an entrepreneur, and how does it help you persevere?

Marketing is 50 percent data and 50 percent gut. There aren't many ways to train your "gut feel" except for jumping right in. Occasionally,

I would run a contest (which is sometimes unknown to the team) putting my gut against the team members or best market practices.

How have you used a book for your business?

If ebooks count, yes. I ghostwrite most of our materials, or at least dictate the content that goes in.

How do you make money from your books? How do you ensure this will continue to happen?

Up-sell, down-sell, and sideways-sell funnels built within a book. Books themselves are like expensive business cards. They don't have to make money up front, but they have to win a second chance at making an impression.

If you lost everything—your book, your list, your products, your platform, your fame—and nobody knew who you were, what would you do in the next 30 days to get back on track, and what role would a book or publication take in the process?

I'll publish only short articles on topics that already have traction. For instance, I'll go to BuzzSumo to see what's trending, hijack the topic, and write my two cents. Then I'll test it on social media to gauge responses and reactions. If it works, I expand or go deep. Then I'll introduce a Call To Action (CTA).

You can reach Kenny at joeyyap.com.

32

DON'T BE AFRAID TO PIVOT BY PAUL BRODIE

What is your business?

Book Publishing and Book Launch Marketing.

What have been the key factors to your success and why?

Main thing is to not be afraid to pivot. Originally, I wanted to utilize my books to give motivational seminars. After my third book, *Positivity Attracts*, became my third best-seller, something changed. I started to have readers and fellow authors contact me. They asked if I could help them share their story about getting the book published and about the book launch. I immediately said yes.

Over the next 18 months, I coached people with their books while still teaching full time. I made the decision at that point to leave my teaching position and focus on coaching people through sharing their stories. Then something changed! I started to work with many business owners who did not want to learn how to publish and market their books. Instead, they wanted to pay me to do it for them and were happy to pay much more as it saved them time and effort by having someone who had a proven system.

That was when I pivoted once again after listening to my clients and providing what they needed. Do not be afraid to pivot as it may be the best thing for your future success.

What is an unusual habit you have as an entrepreneur and how does it help you persevere?

My somewhat unusual habit is to play video games at least an hour a day. It took over two years to realize that I needed an outlet to relax and to not be such a workaholic. I used to think that playing video games was not productive and a waste of time. Since dedicating time daily to play, my stress level is much lower, I have more focus, and can take a temporary mental vacation from my publishing business. It increases my productivity and gives me a new perspective by taking that mental break.

Whether it is working out, relaxing in your pool, or by playing video games, you need to have a way to decompress. I did not realize this until only a few months ago as I was always working on the weekdays and was getting tired constantly.

Video games are a great way to relax and to refocus. I have a retro arcade in my home. One area is a retro arcade machine that has over one thousand arcade games, and the other area plays console games from Nintendo, Sega Genesis, XBOX, PlayStation, and much more. My retro arcade is where I go to decompress, especially after a stressful day as we all have them at times.

You must find an outlet to decompress because if you do not have that outlet then you can burnout quickly.

How have you used a book for your business?

As a publisher, my books are a critical part of my business. I always say that your book in the foundation of your business platform. It is your base, your core, and helps you build stronger relationships with current clients and helps turn potential prospects into clients. Out of my 15 books, the main ones I utilize for business are *Get Published* and *Podcast 101*.

Get Published is great for those getting started in their author journey, especially if you are a business owner who wants to use your book to help build your business. The book covers specific techniques for leveraging the Kindle, paperback, and audiobook version of your book for lead generation. After you have a book then the next step up is having your own podcast. *Podcast 101* details how to complete that journey as the book and the podcast build upon each other.

I utilize both books to help show people how they can leverage their books and then a potential podcast to continue to build their businesses.

How do you make money from your books? How do you ensure this will continue to happen?

One thing I always tell my publishing clients is that you will rarely make a fortune with royalties. There are millions of books on Amazon and the competition is fierce. We focus on one main thing.

That main thing is the back end. Leveraging your book to get readers to set up strategy sessions with the client and offering coaching, consulting, and public speaking and doing book signings. There are many ways to monetize a book, and what we do is show our clients how to leverage the books to take their businesses to the next level and to also make the investment back as soon as possible.

With my own books, I make on average four figures per month in royalties and that is through having 15 books with each available in Kindle, paperback, and audio. We use Amazon Marketing Services to advertise the books as well.

My main business is on the back end, and we have made over six figures on the back end with our publishing company.

What bad advice do you often hear on the subject of authorship or writing a book for your business?

My biggest pet peeve is with fly-by-night publishing gurus who promise people the moon and stars and never deliver. They will promise that you will make lots of money in royalties and never teach you how to properly leverage a book. Main thing is that you must run your book like a business and treat it like a product launch and not just rely on royalties as relying on just royalties is a recipe for disaster.

If you lost everything—your book, your list, your products, your platform, your fame—and nobody knew who you were, what would you do in the next 30 days to get back on track, and what role would a book or publication take in the process?

I would start a new podcast and also create a brand-new eBook about 25 ways to monetize your book. The eBook would be a lead magnet on my website. I would direct traffic to my website through the intro and outro of my podcast. Would also connect to my target market on LinkedIn by offering the guide.

Once they opt in to the guide, the thank-you page would have an invitation to set up a complimentary, no-pitch strategy session to talk about the person's book and how we could potentially help them.

I would also team up with other authors in my network on doing a live webinar through a joint venture. In addition, I would put together a free book promotion with at least ten authors that we would all cross promote for list building.

You can reach Paul at getpublishedsystem.com.

TAKE PRODUCT LAUNCHES TO THE NEXT LEVEL BY JEFF BREWER

My name is Jeff Brewer. I am the creator and founder of the digital marketing company, Launch Hackers Lab. We teach entrepreneurs how to take their product launches to the next level by hacking the product launches of the top marketers in the world and teaching their expert strategies.

I've been running a digital marketing agency since 2012, and in the last few years, I've been helping entrepreneurs focus on scaling their product launches to the next level. I have done a bunch of six-figure, and even seven-figure, launches in the last few years, but this one was probably the most fun.

I want to get into a little background about the client, then show you guys what the top three takeaways are right now. Her name is Annie Grace. Annie worked in a corporate world where coworkers wanted to get together and mingle after work.

When she was visiting a client or a prospect or a vendor in another city, they often invited her to come get a drink at dinner or meet them at the bar. She was doing this, and she was doing it frequently—every day that she was on the road, she was invited for a drink after work. And one drink led to two, which led to three, and so on and so forth.

One day she found herself, like the story goes, on the ground passed out in her hotel room. She had an epiphany: This is not me. I'm becoming a person I'm not. Alcohol is getting the best of me. I really need to stop doing this. I need to stop drinking. I'm going to give up alcohol.

She was not an alcoholic, necessarily, in her mind, but she drank so much socially it became a problem—you've heard the term "functioning alcoholic."

Annie wrote a book called *The Snake in Mind* around this concept. She wasn't aiming for the Alcoholics Anonymous target customer, if you will, but more of this corporate social drinker on the road who might be going through her same situation. It could resonate with that person.

The book blew up, and it was really exciting to see. She started helping a bunch of people. Two years later, she wanted to take this to the next level, which she did by launching a new book called *The Alcohol Experiment*.

The book is written in challenge format. Every chapter in the book is a different challenge. The beauty of this was we were going to start introducing our launch strategy number one, which is merging launches. This is a strategy I use in every single launch.

Instead of doing just the Product Launch Formula (PLF) or just the Perfect Webinar, it's combining different strategies into one launch with doing what we call a challenge launch.

The challenge launch is amazing. It's a launch I'm really geeking out on. I want you to pay attention to how the challenge launch works and how you can merge the challenge launch and stack it as well.

We'll talk about launch stacking with other types of launches to really warm up your audience, add a disproportionate amount of value to them, and get them to raise their hands—not just as an email subscriber, but as a customer and buyer.

Essentially, you could go to Amazon and buy her book for $30 or you could purchase a ticket to the Alcohol Experiment Challenge. We priced that Alcohol Experiment Challenge at $97. When you buy the challenge, you get the book as well—so it's like, hey, you could buy the book or you can get the book with the challenge. Because the book in challenge format, it makes sense. They buy entry into the challenge.

Well, this concept also works if the book isn't written in challenge format. When I say it's written in challenge format, I mean the chapters tell you daily information: Every day you read it, you take the information, think about this mindset, then do this action or some type of assignment. We mapped the challenge around the new year, when people had a New Year's resolution. It was the best time for us to launch the book.

So again, I think, if you're self-publishing your book on Amazon, this can definitely work. You can sell the challenge separately and then have them buy the book. I think the best way to do this is self-publishing and doing a free-plus-shipping book offer where you give your book away for free and then upselling the challenge. Or just selling the challenges and upselling the book. Self-publishing is always going to be the way I recommend people go.

The secret sauce here is after people purchase the $97 challenge, they're getting a substantial amount of value. You then can invite them to a closed and private Facebook group in which you give them things to do in the book—or in some type of workbook—or exercises every day.

And then I want you to be posting, documenting your journey—whether it's journaling, posting videos on social media, or just posting your updates, what you're feeling, what you're thinking, how you're feeling, what results you are getting. One percent of your audience, depending on how good you are, will report back to you. You can document a success story from them at the very end.

I always say launches are not about the revenue you can make but the people you can help. And the more people you can help, the more success stories you can document, the more you'll be able to remarket those success stories and get more people coming into your community on an ongoing basis. It's always about success stories. The more people you can help, the more people you can impact, and the more we can change this world, one person at a time.

They're going to get the transformation because they actually consume the content, which most of the time is the hardest part. The hardest part isn't selling your course membership. It's getting people to actually consume the content, take action, and get the result. The stronger the community and the bigger the transformation, the more people who will want to keep learning from you, keep working with you.

I'm in this amazing community of like-minded individuals who also just graduated the program and the challenge, and they're feeling the same thing I felt. I don't have the fear of missing out by not joining. I feel great. I feel my energy is up. I want to make sure that I don't relapse, if you will, and go back into the state of drinking. How do I keep this woman going? Whenever you deliver a disproportionate amount of value to your audience for a low amount of money, they're going to want more of that. They are going to become addicted to your content, your community, and your engagement.

So why do you sell the challenge for a low amount of money if you're delivering such great value? The reason is because as great marketers and entrepreneurs, we always want to be thinking two or three launches down the road. Don't just think about the fastest and quickest cash grab. Think about how to deliver a disproportionate amount of value to the audience so they want to keep consuming content on an ongoing basis and stay engaged and stay a part of the community. This transitions perfectly into the strategy number two: launch stacking.

You've heard about launch stacking. However, in this case, we're going to start with merging the challenge launch with the book launch, and then after the 30-day challenge is complete, we're then going to stack the next launch on top of it.

Then you'll deliver the sales video on Day 13, which will open your cart for a week. However, in the challenge plus the book launch, you're just doing a challenge launch. The 30-day challenge period has a final training video. That's equivalent to your first three videos in your four-part video series. So you don't necessarily need to take people through the same PLC one, two, and three videos that you would in your four-part video series.

Instead of taking them through another free content series, take the buyers, who we have already introduced to the next thing, and stack the next launch. Send them into our next program. Tell them, "I have great news for you. I want to tell you it's just the beginning. I have an amazing free live training."

This live training is going to be a webinar in which you're going to educate, storytell, add value, and share results from other past students who have gone through your core offer. You're going to sell them on this webinar in your core offer, which is your membership community or digital course.

I've seen this happen in multiple successful challenge launches. You'll see a substantial amount of people who registered for the challenge, bought the challenge, and completed the challenge who are going to attend this live training. It means even more buyers. So one of my good friends and clients that did this launch; she was getting, you know, a pretty standard 20 percent show-up rate on the live webinars; she had about, you know, 5 percent to 10 percent of people out of the 20 percent that were attending were buying. And then she would double it on the replay.

However, when she stacked the webinar after the 30-day challenge, 80 percent of the people that went through the challenge and bought the challenge attended this live training. Out of the 80 percent who joined that webinar live training, 20 percent of them purchased her thousand-dollar course.

This is the strategy to break into the six-figure/seven-figure launches. Instead of Annie just selling her course for $97, of the 3,000 people who came in, let's say, conservatively, only 10 percent attended the live training. She just made another $300,000 (300 times a thousand). Then, let's say she did the Perfect Webinar launch. Almost $600,000 in 32 days.

Do you guys see how powerful that is? Do you see how this could work in your business?

Is that amazing? Do you see the difference of doing something like that and getting actual buyers as opposed to just getting someone to, you know, download a lead magnet? These are people that have paid money, so they're going to put in the work; they're going to take action.

You're going to be able to deliver the transformation; and they're going to become a part of this community; and they're going to become addicted to your content. They're going to want more; and you're going to give it to them. And this format—this merging launches and stacking launch strategy—is going to be the way you take your business from wherever you're at now to six figures and maybe even seven figures. You won't just do this challenge launch once.

You can do it over and over and over again, bringing in new audiences. This is a revolutionary launch strategy that has changed the way I run launches. I think it's going to change the launch game. I still to this day haven't seen a better strategy to deliver this disproportionate amount of value and get people in your community. So I highly, highly recommend everyone at least try it once and see how you can improve it over time.

The final strategy number three we did is joint venture launches and joint venture partners. I think it's a very daunting task for a lot of people to think about, especially when they're just starting out. But just focus on the now. Think about how can you leverage partners that are big—not just individual entrepreneurs, but big media destinations, online destinations, social media influencers. Think about how to collaborate with them, create content with them, interview them on your podcast, YouTube channel, blog, and see if they can reciprocate the favor.

Annie obviously established expertise and a great community from her first book. A great example of this is the best publication we were featured in: *Good Morning America*. It was amazing. Because this movement of *The Alcoholic Experiment* was so successful, she was able to get featured on *Good Morning America*. And you know, we have the call to action there to have people check out the book, and the book led to the challenge, right? So not just stacking interviews and media and podcasts or blogs or Facebook Lives or Instagram Lives or social media influencers, but maybe even local TV stations. Whatever you can do.

We are reaching out to people who had audiences and followings, the people who would purchase your product or want to follow you as well, right? And that's how you leverage the audiences that already exist. That way you don't have to try to organically grow your audience on your own. I think that's a great shortcut.

Give them a call to action—in this case, the book to the challenge, right? Make sure there's a call to action to get people who are consuming your content for free on the interview to hear you, hear the value, then go to your domain.

The next level needs to come so you can plan your biggest events. Again, for Annie, we are taking advantage of the event of New Year's resolutions happening on January 1st. It's the perfect time for *The Alcohol Experiment,* perfect time for people to give up drinking. It was a huge, huge, amazing result.

If you are launching a book specifically and you have it in a free-plus-shipping offer format, you can promise anyone who's promoting it a 40-percent commission and do some type of joint venture launch for them to promote the book for you. So they're incentivized to interview you and to put you into their audience so you pay them a commission for any sales in that free-plus-shipping book offer.

You want to be the market outlier. You want to be the person who delivers the most value in your market so people become addicted to your content and keep coming back to you time and time again. Become the top launcher in your space—in your community. I want you to think about how you can use these strategies in your next slump.

So as a recap, remember, merge strategies together. Don't be scared to get creative. Strategy number two, stack your launches. And strategy number three, use drive venture partners. Use media to leverage the power of PR and social media to promote your core offer for your challenge or book launch. Create friendships and relationships first. The business partnership will come after that. Always be thinking about how to deliver a disproportionate amount of value to your customers and your partners.

Use these three launch strategies of merging, stacking your launches, and leveraging the power of joint venture partners in PR, and I promise you your launches will go to a level you never dreamed was possible. You'll get faster results. You'll become the category king or queen and the thought leader in your space, in your industry. And I promise you your launches will never see the kind of successful results that they will when implementing these strategies. You're always one launch away.

THE NETFLIX OF SELF-PUBLISHING

Want your book to be a Bestseller?
How about maximizing distribution?
What about marketing, video, ads and podcasting?

You don't need to buy every course out there to accomplish your goals. You can borrow them with bookflix.tv for an extremely economical month to month tuition.

Bookflix.tv provides all access learning to all the courses you need, with video tutorials, worksheets and templates:

- Learn how to quickly and easily plan and write your your first draft

- Think Amazon will give you the **maximum distribution for your book?** Think again. We show you how in the Draft to Published Roadmap class.
- Will hitting **Amazon Bestseller** put your book on autopilot? No. Follow this launch plan and build a consistent marketing plan (and hit bestseller with ease).
- How to know exactly which ads will get you the most traffic without guessing
- The exact method to stack ads (if you don't do this, Amazon won't show your book to anyone)
- We are adding more courses from the instructors you love everyday!

Go check it out now!

https://www.bookflix.tv